The Discerning Heart

The Developmental Psychology of Robert Kegan

Philip M Lewis

Acknowledgements:

Cover art and design by:
Benjamin Lewis

Editorial assistance provided by:
Louise Katainen
Joyce Rothschild

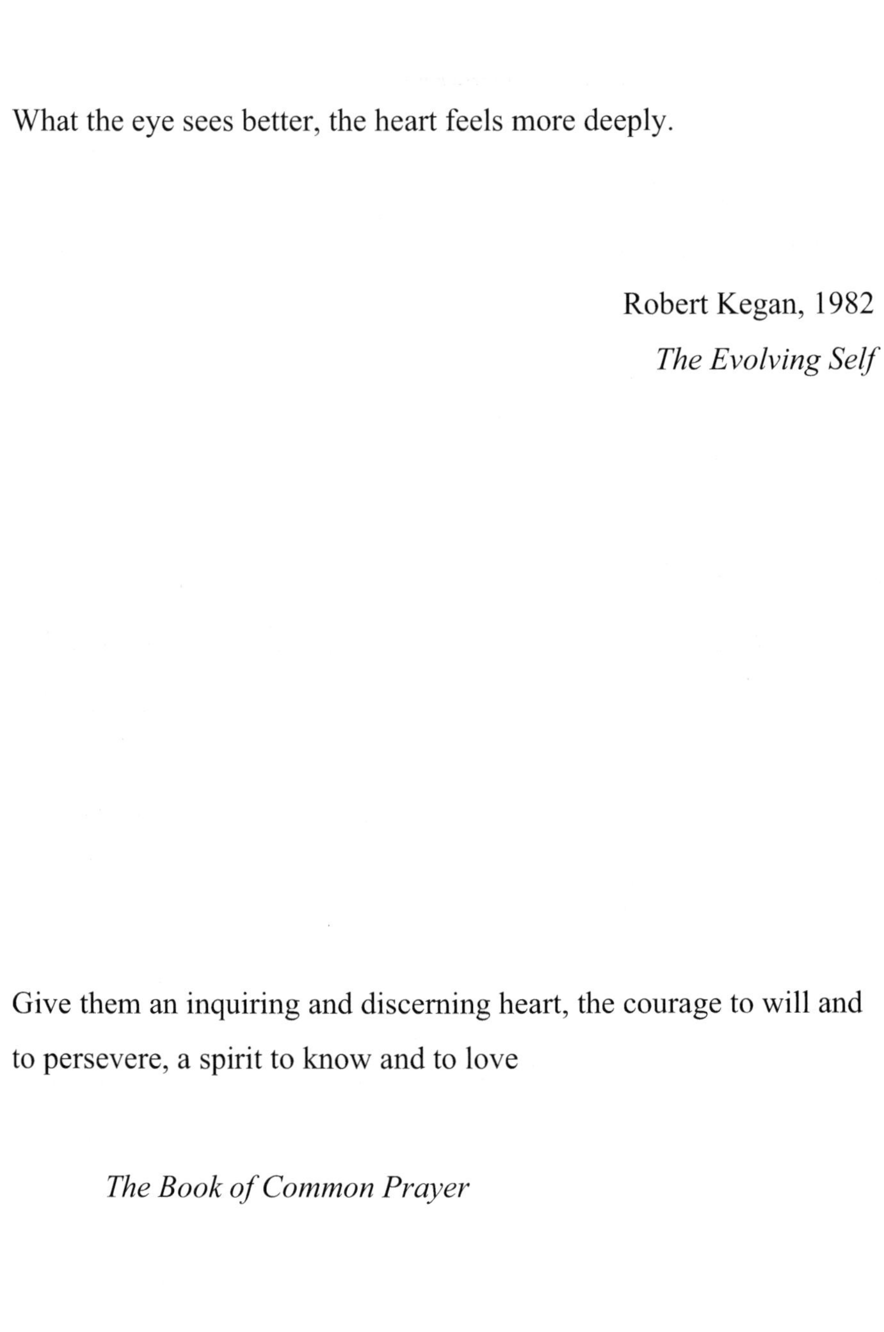

What the eye sees better, the heart feels more deeply.

Robert Kegan, 1982
The Evolving Self

Give them an inquiring and discerning heart, the courage to will and to persevere, a spirit to know and to love

The Book of Common Prayer

Table of Contents

1 INTRODUCTION 6

2 HOW JEAN PIAGET CHANGED THE WAY WE SEE OURSELVES 8

3 KEGAN'S CONSTRUCTIVE/DEVELOPMENTAL THEORY OF THE SELF 27

4 STAGE 2: LET'S MAKE A DEAL 42

5 STAGE 3 – CREATING AN INTERPERSONAL SELF 52

6 STAGE 3 THOUGHT ALSO CREATES A NEW KIND OF SUBJECTIVE EXPERIENCE 67

7 STAGE 4: A SELF-AUTHORED IDENTITY 80

8 STAGE 5: BEYOND PSYCHOLOGICAL AUTONOMY 96

9 THE DYNAMICS OF DEVELOPMENTAL CHANGE 101

10 A GOOD HOLDING ENVIRONMENT ALSO ENTAILS STICKING AROUND 109

11 DEVELOPMENTAL CHANGE IS INHERENTLY STRESSFUL 113

12 KEGAN'S THEORY HELPS EXPLAIN MANY ASPECTS OF CLOSE RELATIONSHIPS 126

13 CONCLUDING THOUGHTS 134

1 INTRODUCTION

This small book is about how, if we are fortunate, we get smarter as we grow older. Smarter, not in the sense that our IQ score rises, but smarter in a much more important sense. This book is about the growth of human understanding, a kind of understanding that enables us to see both ourselves and others more clearly and, in the process, leads us to feel more deeply. Its focus is a remarkable new theory of the development of the self by Harvard psychologist Robert Kegan. Having spent the past 25 years teaching others about Kegan's vision of human development and investigating the role of psychological maturity in leader effectiveness, I am confident that the ideas contained in this book will enable you to view yourself, others, and the world through new eyes. It will put your experience of living in the world in motion and, I hope, make you both more discerning and thereby more vulnerable to our very human struggle of making sense of our lives.

Here are some of the ways this may happen. You will begin to better understand why your adolescent or adult children, even though they are physically adults, sometimes act in ways that you see so clearly as showing poor judgment. You will better understand why your boss or some of your co-workers "just don't get it" when critical situations arise at work, even though the issues are perfectly clear to you. And some of you will discover how someone you have loved for many years seems to have become stuck in outworn views of the world, while you have gradually become more discerning. Or, perhaps, how that person has gradually become more self-confident and more discerning, and you are the one who has become stuck in a psychologically familiar but incomplete understanding of yourself and others. Most importantly, this book will impart a cautious optimism about the lack of shared understanding that these situations describe, because you will come to see many important human differences as manifestations of people occupying different points along a continuum of psychological growth. With time, and some psychological "work," most of those who are lagging a bit behind will catch up and you will get them back, or more precisely get them forward, in a reprise of that wonderful experience where a child or adolescent whom you love begins to see things more clearly and completely and joins you, for the first time, in a psychological world you have been occupying for some time.

This is pointedly not a book of familiar ideas dressed up in new clothes. Kegan's ideas are neither obvious nor easy, so grasping his views of identity development will take some effort. I wish this were not so. But if Kegan's vision of our lifelong journey of making sense of our experience were simple or obvious, then you would already be using it to think about yourself and others. Kegan's ideas are transformative precisely because they provide a new and more sophisticated lens for bringing the universal human struggle for sense making into better focus, a lens that will begin to help you knit together your past, your present, and your future with more clarity and sympathy.

2 HOW JEAN PIAGET CHANGED THE WAY WE SEE OURSELVES

We are all psychologists. In order to manage ourselves and our relationships we develop theories that help us predict how others are going to react to us and how we can get others (and ourselves) to behave in desired ways. This need to understand human behavior is one reason people are drawn to psychology classes and self-help psychology books. But when we look to both popular psychology and its academic basis to try to improve our understanding, we find that there are a variety of psychological theories from which to choose, each with a particular take on human nature. Reflecting the lack of a single unifying theory in the field of psychology, these various approaches are often quite different in their description of what animates us. Take, for example, the contrasting view of human experience found in Freudian and Jungian psychoanalytic theory versus that found in Skinnerian behavioral theory. Sigmund Freud and Carl Jung viewed human beings as possessing a vast psychological unconscious, hidden from ordinary awareness, out of which flow our desires and passions. B. F. Skinner, in contrast, asserted that it is not what lies hidden in our mind that determines who we are and how we experience the world. The only thing that really matters, according to Skinner, is the structure of our external environment. It is the environment, Skinner argued, not some fictional unconscious mind, that profoundly shapes our actions (and thereby our experiences). Despite their obvious differences, both approaches minimize the role of rational choice in human behavior. Freud and Jung believed that much of our experience is generated by unconscious urges over which we exert little or no conscious control. Skinner discounted the role of choice entirely, viewing us as unwitting products of our immediate and past environmental circumstances. These contrasting psychologies have differing implications for many things, including, for example, how we achieve self-mastery. For Freud and Jung, we gain greater control over our lives and ourselves as we discover and harness more of that which lies in our unconscious minds. For Skinner we become more effective as we discover and manage the environmental forces that so powerfully control our behavior. While both these views of human nature are useful, neither reflects the underlying view of human nature that animates this book. Robert Kegan's view of human development flows from a third theoretical tradition. Kegan traces the origin of his ideas about the development of the self to the constructive developmental theory of the Swiss psychologist Jean Piaget.

The ideas of Jean Piaget have had a lasting impact on the fields of developmental psychology and childhood education. And even though some particulars and details of his discoveries have been questioned by contemporary researchers, the broad outlines of Piaget's approach to understanding cognitive development have endured. Piaget scholar David Elkind puts it thus:

> Just as Freud's discoveries of unconscious motivation, infantile sexuality, and the stages of psychosexual growth changed our way of thinking about human personality, so Piaget's discoveries of children's implicit philosophies or systems of beliefs, the construction of reality by the infant, and the stages of mental development have altered our ways of thinking about human intelligence.[1]

This is not, of course, a book about "human intelligence." But Robert Kegan has extended Piaget's view of intelligence into the area of identity formation and identity development. In doing so, Kegan has harnessed Piagetian theory in a way that avoids the deterministic views of human nature found in both psychoanalytic and behavioral theories. Let's take a look at what Kegan saw in Piaget's ideas that led to his new formulation of identity development.

We'll start with what it means to state that Piaget's and Kegan's theories are "constructive-developmental. Consider the "constructivist" piece first. Contructivists assert that we do not passively respond to the "objective" circumstances of our lives. Instead we actively "construct" or organize those circumstances into a meaningful whole. We then respond in terms of our internally created view of our circumstances, not directly to the objective properties of those circumstances. This tendency to construct a personal, subjective reality rather than respond to an objective reality is one reason two people who find themselves in identical circumstances can have such different experiences of those circumstances. You may recall that despite the fact that we all watched the same murder trial on television, white viewers generally thought O. J. Simpson was guilty of the murder of his ex-wife Nicole Brown while most African American viewers generally believed him to be innocent. Objectively, we all heard the same testimony and evidence, but subjectively we were not living in the same world at all. We had constructed different realities. What makes this view particularly important to a better understanding of others and ourselves is the fact that we generally are unaware of the fact that we have actively constructed the meaning we attach to our experiences. Instead, we assume that what we "see" is what is objectively there. As you will see shortly, Kegan demonstrates how the capacity to be aware of and take responsibility for the reality we have constructed for ourselves is a developmental achievement.

The constructivist view reminds us that no one lives in the same reality, and if we want to communicate effectively with others, we need to keep this in mind. Most approaches to diversity training are based on this insight. But as useful as it is to realize that everyone constructs his or her own reality differently, by itself this "constructivist" position (as well as most diversity training) has only modest utility. It can easily degenerate into a view that everyone is different, or everyone is unique. At best, a purely constructivist view of human experience reminds us to pay close attention to what others say and do, because chances are they have a somewhat different take on what's going on than we do. A somewhat more useful sort of constructivism results from approaches that group people with respect to how they construct reality. By sorting people into different groups or categories, we don't have to diagnose each individual's unique construction of reality. Instead, we need only to remind ourselves, for example, that women are from Venus while men are from Mars[2] or that our boss is an intuitive thinker while we are a sensing feeler.[3]

Fortunately, Piaget's theory of the development of human intelligence was more than a constructivist theory; it was also a developmental theory. And it is this Piagetian combination of constructivism and developmentalism that generates much of the power of Kegan's view of human experience. Piaget discovered that there are a limited number of increasingly complex ways of constructing reality. He called these eras or stages. Each is based on a certain underlying logic or way of organizing our experiences, and each successive stage builds upon and incorporates developmentally earlier stages. The explanatory power of combining the constructivist notion with the notion that there are a limited number of qualitative shifts in how reality is constructed can be illustrated by considering one of Piaget's famous demonstrations. The demonstration illustrates how differently two children at adjacent developmental stages construct an understanding of physical reality. If you have access to children of the right ages, you can try this out for yourself.

Present a three- or four-year-old and a seven- or eight-year-old with the following situation: On a table in front of the child place three glasses. Two should be identical short, wide glasses and the third a tall, narrow glass (it helps if the sides of the taller glass are also thicker than the sides of the two shorter, wider glasses). Fill the two short glasses with an identical amount of liquid. Leave the tall, narrow glass empty. Now ask each child (out of the presence of the other) "is there the same amount of liquid (Kool-Aid, etc.) in the two glasses or does one have more?" Not surprisingly, both the younger and the older child will answer that there is the same amount in each glass. Next, while the child is watching, pour the liquid from one of the short, wide glasses into the tall, narrow glass. For the demonstration to work, it helps if the level of the liquid is noticeably higher in the narrow glass. Repeat your original question. The result is likely to be that the older child answers that there is the same amount of liquid in the two differently shaped glasses. In stark contrast, the younger child is likely to say that there is more liquid in the tall, narrow glass. Reversing the procedure, by pouring the liquid back into the empty short glass and then back into the tall glass a second time, doesn't alter the younger child's belief that when the liquid is in the taller, narrower glass there is more of it than there is when it is in the shorter, wider glass. How can we understand this dramatic age difference? What causes the typical four-year-old to make such an error of judgment? What enables the eight-year-old to provide the correct answer?

Your first inclination may be to say that the older child has had more experience with such things than has the younger child. And you would, of course, likely be correct. But how do you explain the fact that even when the younger child is shown that the liquid can be returned to an amount equal to what is in the other short, wide glass she/he still believes that if it *looks* like there is more liquid in the taller glass, then there *is* more liquid. Shouldn't the child's immediate experience with what Piaget called "reversibility" teach the child that merely changing how something looks doesn't alter how much of it there is? Not according to Piaget. Piaget showed through numerous simple but ingenious demonstrations of the sort depicted here how intellectual understanding is a joint function of both experience *and* the complexity of one's cognitive "construction" of that experience. In Piaget's view, the younger child lacks the cognitive capacity to make her/his perceptions of the liquid (it really does look like there is more in the taller glass) the focus of a more complex and encompassing cognitive structure. Experience counts, according to Piaget, but only if it results in a more complicated (and adequate) way of structuring that experience. The older child has evidently done this while the younger child has not. The younger child seems to live in a very impermanent universe, where changes in how things look are taken to be changes in the thing itself. The older child, in contrast, lives in a much more stable and "concrete" universe, one made more stable by her/his capacity to "conserve" the essential nature of things even when how they look changes. Elkind describes the achievement of the older child as illustrative of a key proposition of Piaget's theory.

> The essence of the theory can be simply stated: the child discovers conservation - permanence across apparent change- with the aid of reason. It is by reasoning about his experience that the (older) child is able to overcome illusions and discover how things really are.[4]

The older child in the conservation demonstration has the same perceptions as the younger child. Even to the older child, it looks like there is more liquid in the taller glass. But, unlike the younger child, the older child can *reason about* what she/he perceives. And that new reasoning capacity, the hallmark of Piaget's higher developmental stage (the "concrete operational stage"), permits the older child to construct a more adequate understanding of physical reality.

But what, you might ask, does all of this have to do with identity development, which is the focus of Kegan's theory? Doesn't Piaget's demonstration merely show that older children are better thinkers than younger children? Where, exactly, is the news in this? Here's where Kegan weighed in. What if, Kegan asked, this simple demonstration of a developmental difference in cognitive capacity is an instance of a more general feature of personality development? Part of the genius of Robert Kegan was that he both saw and articulated this idea. To illustrate this extension of Piaget's theory into the area of personality and identity, let's consider a seemingly very different situation. Again, we have two children, ages four and eight. This time imagine they are brothers at home with their mom and dad on a Saturday morning. Four-year-old Jimmy comes downstairs to find his mother about to bake cookies. She invites him to help, and he is delighted to do so. Just as they are getting started, Jimmy's dad comes in and says he's going out to run a few errands. Knowing how much Jimmy loves spending time with him, he invites Jimmy along. Jimmy eagerly accepts and proceeds out to the car with his dad. But as they start to back out of the driveway, Jimmy begins to cry. Surprised, his dad asks Jimmy what's wrong? "I wanted to bake cookies with mom," he replies through his tears. "That's fine," says his dad and sends him back into the house, where he takes up his place next to his mom in the kitchen. But no sooner has he done so than he again bursts into tears. "What's wrong?" his mother asks. "I wanted to go in the car with dad." Odd as this scenario sounds to people unfamiliar with toddlers, this phenomenon is common enough in young children that the child psychoanalyst, Margaret Mahler, gave it a name, "ambitendency," to distinguish it from a developmentally more advanced phenomenon that we call ambivalence.[5]

Now consider Jimmy's eight-year-old brother, Antoine. He too likes to help his mom bake cookies, and he also likes to go out to run errands with his dad. Now imagine that Antoine is faced with the same situation his younger brother faced. Just as he is beginning to help his mom bake cookies, his dad invites Antoine to go with him in the car. What does Antoine do in this situation? We can be pretty sure that eight-year-old Antoine is not going to repeat his little brother's behaviors. Instead, Antoine will likely do one of the following: He may think about his two options - bake cookies, go with his dad - and decide which one he would rather do. Or, liking to do both, he may try to get one or the other of his parents to delay one activity until he has finished the other. That way he'll be able to do both. In any event, he's not going to burst into tears. Clearly Antoine is acting more maturely than his little brother. How can we make sense of this age difference, and how does it resemble what Piaget illuminated with his conservation demonstration?

Recall how Piaget explained a similar age/stage difference in the conservation demonstration. Piaget asserted that the critical developmental difference between the two children in his demonstration was that the older child was able to *reason about* his perceptions of the liquid whereas the younger child was unable to do so. (Brain cramp alert: I'm about to use two technical terms that are central to understanding Kegan's ideas.) Piaget would say that the older child was able to "decenter" from his perceptions while the younger child was "embedded" in those perceptions. Another way of saying this is to talk about differences in perspective. The older child has a *perspective on* his perception that there is more liquid in the taller, narrower glass. The younger child lacks that perspective.

If it looks like there is more liquid to the younger child, then there is more!

Now consider the possibility that Piaget's analysis might also illuminate the differing reactions of little Jimmy and his older brother, Antoine. First off, we don't appear to be dealing here with differing *perceptions* of the physical world. Instead, what is most salient for the two brothers are two immediate *desires*, a desire to help mom bake cookies and a desire to run errands with dad. Both boys have both desires, but their responses to those desires are very different. Following the logic of Piaget's analysis of the conservation demonstration, could it be that the older child is able to "reason about" his desires while the younger child cannot? Stated in terms of perspectives, perhaps the older boy can take a perspective on ("decenter" from) his competing desires while the younger boy is "embedded" in one or the other of his desires, and thus cannot step back from and contemplate or mentally weigh his two desires. This could explain much about the brothers' different reactions. His mother's invitation to bake cookies activates in little Jimmy a desire to help. Then his father's invitation to go out activates a desire to go out with his dad. Because he is embedded in each desire *in turn* (he only has one desire at a time), Jimmy wants what he wants when he wants it. Once in the car with dad, little Jimmy's thoughts turn to his mom baking cookies in the kitchen. That thought reactivates his desire to bake cookies. About to be separated from the opportunity to bake cookies, he starts crying. Returning to the house, he soon realizes his dad is leaving to run errands without him, so his desire to go with his dad is reactivated, and he once again bursts into tears. What's going on here is that little Jimmy experiences his two desires one desire at a time. Just as Piaget's younger subject in the conservation demonstration could only experience the situation through his immediate perception (first the amounts looked the same; then it looked like there was more liquid in the taller glass), here Jimmy can only experience his situation through an immediate desire or "impulse." Not so for his older brother. Antoine is able to recognize that he has two competing desires, and he demonstrates this capacity when he weighs them both together to see which he'd most like to do. In doing so Antoine is *reasoning about*, and is demonstrating his ability to *take a perspective on* his two desires. To use one of Piaget's terms, Antoine is able to "decenter" from his two desires and take a broader view ("How can I get both of the things I want out of this situation?").

My hope is that the above example illustrates how Piaget's theoretical analysis of developmental differences in children's *intellectual* understanding can be broadened and used to clarify phenomenon usually subsumed under *personality* dynamics - in this instance how children at two different developmental stages manage competing desires. As you will see shortly, Kegan takes this neo-Piagetian analysis even further and uses it not only to illuminate intrapsychic (internal) experiences of the sort described above but also to clarify the complexities of human relationships.

You may have noticed that the two examples used above both concern children. And you may wonder how Kegan's use of Piaget's concepts could be applied to adults. As an illustration of how this was accomplished, let's consider one last example. Imagine that you are involved in a close relationship where conflicts periodically arise around issues of being on time. From time to time each of you has failed to show up when you were supposed to, and this has caused hard feelings. On the present occasion you are the one who is late, and when you finally do arrive, you can see that your friend is quite angry. Seeing his anger, you immediately get a sick feeling in the pit of your stomach. And until he is no longer angry with you, you feel awful. So you launch into apologies and explanations and assurances that it won't happen again. If that fails to reduce his anger, you try to engage him in a more pleasant activity so that he'll start enjoying being with you again rather than being angry with you. If nothing works, you'll continue to feel awful. Just knowing that he's still mad at you is enough to threaten your sense of personal equilibrium.

Now contrast the above example of how you each react when you keep him waiting to how things go when he keeps you waiting. Imagine that for the third time in the past month he has failed to show up on time to take you to your exercise class. You know that he knows that you like to be there on time and that you particularly hate having to walk in late in front of your classmates. Waiting for him to show up, you begin to wonder if he takes you for granted, or worse, doesn't care about you as much as he used to. These thoughts only make you even more upset. When he finally does arrive, it is clear that his being late has really upset you. How does he react to your being upset? He immediately launches into a detailed explanation of why he was late and tries to talk you into seeing his side of it. When this gambit doesn't work (because for you the main issue is how his feelings for you may have changed) *he* becomes angry with *you* for being upset (the old "the best defense is a good offence" gambit). He tries to convince you that you're making a big deal out of a minor problem, and he suggests that you should "get over it." You end up feeling like you have created an even bigger problem for your relationship by getting upset over his being late, because now he *is* upset with you! You may even secretly admire how easily he goes on the offensive when conflicts like this occur, something you seem constitutionally unable to do. It's pretty clear from the way he's acting that he's not going to get that awful feeling in the pit of *his* stomach, as you did when your roles were reversed.

What's going on here? Why are your experiences and reactions so different from his? Do the two of you merely have two different personality styles, where you're hypersensitive to conflict and he's not? Or might the differences stem from a different level of investment in the relationship? Could it be that the relationship matters a great deal more to you than it does to him? Or perhaps the two of you grew up with different models of conflict resolution in your own families, and as a result the two of you approach conflicts in very different ways. Of course, any or all of these explanations could be true. But Kegan, drawing on Piaget, suggests another, less obvious, but perhaps more illuminating view. Kegan focuses on the possibility that the differences between how you and your friend react may be due to a *developmental* difference between you - a fundamental difference in perspective-taking capacity. Here's how Kegan might analyze these different reactions using his neo-Piagetian perspective. First of all, it's clear that both you and your friend can see things from the other person's perspective. You know that he doesn't like it when you are late, and he knows that you don't like it when he's late. So there's no apparent developmental difference in this regard. You both have the capacity to put yourself in the other's place and to know how the other person might feel, even if that's not the way you would feel. But is there any evidence that either of you can "decenter" from, and take a broader, more complex perspective on, those two individual perspectives? Perhaps yes. Recall that your perception that your friend was angry with you for being late directly affected how you felt about yourself (remember that sick feeling in the pit of your stomach?). Kegan would point out that your emotional reaction is a function of a perspective-taking capacity that is more sophisticated than the capacity merely to see another's point of view as an alternative to your own. (I know this is getting a bit complicated, but don't let your eyes glass over. This is important.) Kegan would suggest that in your response to being kept waiting you demonstrate your capacity to take two perspectives *simultaneously* as opposed to each in turn. Your friend demonstrates no such capacity. In this instance, that simultaneity is seen in the way your perception of how he is experiencing you (one perspective) *becomes a part of* how you experience yourself (another perspective). Both perspectives are experienced *at the same time* and create that awful feeling in the pit of your stomach. That feeling in the pit of your stomach is a function of your experiencing his experience of you. This sounds complicated, and it is. That awful feeling in the pit of your stomach is a simultaneous function of *your* experience of yourself based in part on your awareness of *his* anger towards you. If you're not sure you followed that, don't despair; this somewhat complicated but critically important idea will be further clarified below in the chapter on Kegan's stage 3.

But what about your friend? Does he also demonstrate this capacity to take two perspectives simultaneously? Apparently not. He does, however, demonstrate an ability to see things from two different perspectives. He can see your perspective; he knows you're upset because you hate to be late to your exercise class. And he also sees things from his own perspective. He knows why he was doing the things that made him late. And he also doesn't like it when you are upset. Because when you're upset, you're not much fun to be with. So he's interested in your getting over it. All of the above entails looking at things from one perspective at a time (yours or his). What's missing is any evidence that how *you* perceive him *becomes a part of* how he perceives himself (i.e., in contrast to how you respond, there's no evidence of simultaneous perspective-taking on his part). Instead, what your friend understands to be your perspective (he thinks that you want to be able to count on him to be on time) is seen by him as an *alternative* to his own perspective (he wants you to cut him a little slack). So your friend, understanding the situation from the point of view of these alternative perspectives, tries to convince you that you can trust him to be on time in the future. He thinks that's all you want (you actually want a good deal more), and he becomes angry with you when you seem impervious to his perfectly sincere explanations and promises. If he promises you what you're wanting, then you should reciprocate and give him what he wants (that you "just get over it"). There is nothing in his response that speaks of simultaneous perspective-taking. He does not appear to make your experience of him a part of his own experience of himself. Instead, your being upset with him remains an *external* problem for him that he will try to solve by getting you over being upset. When he fails, he shrugs and moves on, something you can't do until the bad feelings between the two of you are resolved. Indeed, you may even secretly admire his psychological "independence" and wish you weren't so "dependent" on the relationship.

This neo-Piagetian analysis provides a fundamentally different way of looking at these individual differences than one finds in almost every other psychological analysis. Rather than seeing your and your friend's differing reactions to being late as a function of differences in personality *style* (Mars vs. Venus) or differences in the depth of your commitments to the relationship (he's falling out of love with me), your differing reactions can be seen as reflecting a developmental difference in perspective-taking capacity. This new way of understanding what may be going on here has some important implications. For one, you might have to stop seeing your friend's offensive behavior as willfully insensitive, and instead come to see it as reflecting an entirely different level (or stage) of interpersonal understanding. Perhaps, you'd say to yourself, he can't really understand what I'm most upset about, because he doesn't have the perspective-taking capability to "see" it. In other words, maybe it's developmentally too complex for him.

There is a broad similarity here between his not being able to see what you are most upset about and Piaget's four-year-old not being able to "see" that the amount of liquid in a glass doesn't change just because it looks like it does. And perplexed as we may be by the younger child's "error," we recognize that she or he is merely a young child, so we assume the child will get smarter as she or he gets older. But what about the possibility that an *adult* that we know and care about may also have a developmentally simpler way of making sense of his experience than we do? Are we able to content ourselves with the thought that "he'll get smarter as he gets older?" Are we willing to wait until he "grows up"? Once we find ourselves thinking developmentally like this, we are starting down a very different path of what long-term relationships are all about. We begin to realize that long-term relationships are as much about the nurturing of one another's psychological development as they are about compatibility. Because if human beings change in the ways they structure their experiences over the course of their lives, as Kegan suggests, then there will likely be periods in any long-term relationship (not just parent-child relationships) where people function for a time at different levels of understanding. We turn now to Kegan's view of those levels of understanding.

3 KEGAN'S CONSTRUCTIVE/DEVELOPMENTAL THEORY OF THE SELF

In the previous chapter I provided a brief example concerning how you and a friend might make sense of incidents in which each of you has repeatedly failed to show up on time. The example illustrates how different people often "see" similar situations in very different ways. I then suggested you consider the possibility that these differing reactions to being late could result from the fact that you and your friend function at different developmental stages. In particular, I set up the example so that your friend organized his experience of being late in terms of how it impacted his *individual* interests. You, in contrast, organized your experience of his being late in terms of how you experienced his anger (when you were late) or in terms of concern over being taken for granted by him (when he was late). In doing so, I was depicting you as being at a higher (and more complex) developmental stage than your friend. Though exactly what this means has not yet been clarified, your friend would be at Kegan's "stage 2," while your reactions would place you at Kegan's "stage 3." In the present chapter I am going to provide you with a framework for understanding Kegan's stages of development. There are six stages in all, labeled "0" through "5," with stage 5 the highest or most advanced, and stage 0 the most primitive.

One way to begin to understand what Kegan's stages are all about is to think about them as reflecting progressively more complicated perspective-taking capacities. In the above example, your friend demonstrated the important and valuable capacity of being able to take alternative perspectives – seeing what you want versus what he wants. You, however, demonstrated a more complex (and developmentally more advanced) capacity. You were able to hold together two perspectives simultaneously. In the example, your friend is "less advanced" developmentally because he is only able to consider two perspectives, one at a time. Let me remind you how you demonstrated your more complex capacity for simultaneous perspective-taking. Your experience or view of yourself (that's one perspective – you thinking about yourself) was in part determined by how you perceived him reacting toward you (that's a second perspective – his view of you and his attendant anger toward you). But for you, these weren't alternative perspectives (as they would have been for your friend). For you, the first perspective included the second. They were going on simultaneously. You made his anger toward you and his disregard of your feelings a part of your own experience of yourself. In that way, you were demonstrating Kegan's stage 3 capacity for simultaneous perspective taking. Your friend, in contrast, was demonstrating the developmentally earlier stage 2 capacity for alternative perspective taking (i.e., one perspective at a time). Kegan's descriptions of his stages 1 through stage 5 are defined, in part, by progressively more sophisticated perspective-taking capacities. Each successively more complex capacity produces its own characteristic construction of circumstances and associated set of emotional reactions. In short, they are used to "construct" qualitatively more complex ways of experiencing oneself and the world.

Kegan's stage 0, present at birth and evident in early infancy, is presumed to be a period where the infant lacks a true psychological perspective. Internal and external events are not distinguished from one another by the newborn, and everything is just sensory experience. The infant has no real sense of self, because there is no "other" or not-self. In a way, self and everything else are one. Because Kegan is interested in the development of the self, he spends little time describing this earliest stage (stage 0). It is merely the condition or state out of which his stage 1 develops. Let's begin by taking a look at the perspective-taking capacities evident in Kegan's stage 1 and contrasting these with the capacities of someone at stage 2.

Stage 1: The Impulsive Stage and the Subject-Object Distinction

Recall Piaget's four-year-old in his famous conservation demonstration. Unlike the older child, the four-year-old believed that because it looked like there was more liquid in the tall skinny glass, there *was* more liquid. The explanation offered by Piaget for this curious misperception was that the four-year-old was unable to "decenter" from, or take a perspective on, his immediate perceptions. Stated slightly differently, the four-year-old viewed the external world (in this case the liquid in the glass) only *through* his perceptions. This stage-1 four-year-old was not able to make his immediate perception (it looks like there's more liquid) the "object of" a broader perspective. In contrast, Piaget pointed out, the eight-year-old (Kegan's stage 2) could "reason about" his perceptions. It is this deceptively simple analysis, and the general model of human experience that it suggests, that forms the basis of Kegan's theory. It comprises what Kegan terms the subject/object distinction.[6] Understanding the subject/object distinction is central to a general understanding of Kegan's personality theory. Indeed, knowing what is "subject" and what is "object" for a particular individual may be the single most important thing we can know about that individual (and about ourselves!). As Kegan puts it, the subject/object level of an individual is the "deep structure" of that individual's personality.[7] And at times, Kegan refers to his view of the development of the self as "subject-object theory." So to reiterate, Piaget suggests that the stage-1 child is subject to her perceptions – she sees *through* them and cannot make her perceptions the object of a broader organizing process. Piaget's analysis in this instance concerns the status of the child's perceptions. Why, then, did Kegan refer to this stage as the "impulsive" stage and not the perception stage? The answer is that the name reflects Kegan's attempt to broaden and extend Piaget's formulations beyond the construction of the physical world to the world of identity and subjective experience.

You have already encountered an example of how this

reformulation might look in the account of little Jimmy and his older brother Antoine. Jimmy was consumed by his immediate desire, either to bake cookies with his mother (desire 1) or to go to the store with his father (desire 2). It was suggested that Jimmy was "embedded" in each desire *in turn*, and lacked the capacity to "decenter" from, and think about, the two desires *together*. Stated in subject/object terms, little Jimmy was *subject to* his immediate desires, while his older brother, Antione, was able to make his immediate desires the *object of* a broader set of interests. In Kegan's theory, little Jimmy is considered to be in stage 1, his older brother in stage 2. In his 1982 book Kegan labeled little Jimmy's stage the "impulsive stage." This is an apt title in the sense that children in this early childhood stage are embedded in or subject to their immediate desires or impulses. Let's take a look at another example of how this so-called subject/object formulation increases our understanding of the behavior and experience of children at this stage.

Consider the phenomenon of temper tantrums. Imagine that your toddler is tired and hungry. He wants a cookie, and he wants it now. You think a cookie should come after dinner, which you expect to have on the table in a matter of minutes, so you say "no." Things get ugly. Your toddler begins screaming, "I hate you; I wish you were dead!" You find all this screaming and yelling unpleasant, but you console yourself with the idea that your toddler doesn't *really* hate you, he's just saying that because he's tired and hungry or perhaps to manipulate you into producing the desired cookie. Later in the evening, after he's eaten and has had his bath, he's snuggled contentedly on your lap listening to a bedtime story. He looks up at you with those adorable two-year-old's eyes and says "I love you," and you conclude that he didn't really mean those hurtful things he said before supper. Well, guess what? You're probably wrong! If your toddler is in the "impulsive" stage, Kegan's stage 1, he may have been completely candid when he told you he hated you. The hallmark of Kegan's stage 1 is that the child is embedded in his or her *immediate* perceptions, feelings, and impulses. Your toddler can't reflect upon his immediate experiences. Instead, he experiences the physical and interpersonal world *through* what he wants ("impulse") and what he feels. His frustration at being denied a cookie is the "lens" through which he regards and experiences you. Organizing his experience of you through his immediate desire and frustration, he can only "see" you as the person who is denying him what he wants. Embedded in this frustrated desire for a cookie, he indeed hates you. He's not being manipulative (stage-1 children lack the perspective required to be manipulative); he's being "honest." But what about later on, when he's lovingly snuggled on your lap? At that point, he loves you, and that's honest too. What this hypothetical stage-1 child lacks is the capacity to coordinate what he feels at one moment (frustration/hatred) with what he feels at another moment (contentment/love). Stated in the theoretical terms of Kegan's formulation, he lacks the capacity to make his immediate feelings and desires the "object" of a perspective that could hold his feelings of frustration and hatred together with his loving feelings. We, as adults, do this holding together all the time, and so do most school-age children. We may become frustrated when someone we care about disappoints us, but we also continue to know that they care about us. Holding those two ideas together *at the same time*, we are not flooded only with feelings of disappointment or hatred. We feel the disappointment, but we make our immediate disappointment "object"; we are not "subject to" our disappointment. We have a more enduring perspective on the person who has disappointed us, an enduring perception that this person cares about us, thus making "object" our immediate reaction of disappointment.

One thing Kegan's theory reminds us is that we are mistaken when we believe our children think (and feel) the way we do. They don't. Unlike us, the typical toddler's immediate feelings and impulses are "subject." We, in marked contrast, are able to weigh our competing desires, much as Antoine did, when trying to decide between baking cookies and going the store with his dad. You may have done just this sort of weighing of competing desires when you started reading this chapter. Perhaps what you felt like doing was watching TV or going to bed. But you didn't, because you psychologically stepped back from your immediate impulse to do something easy and instead regulated your behavior using a broader frame of reference. So, for example, you may have decided that, in terms of your longer-term interests (getting a better handle on yourself and your close relationships), you would ignore your immediate impulses and desires and instead read this chapter. This capacity to take a perspective on, to decenter from, one's immediate impulses is the capacity that defines the stage immediately beyond the impulsive stage, Kegan's stage 2. But, "Wait a minute," you say. "Is it being suggested that I'm only at Kegan's stage 2?" No. What I am suggesting is that you have available to you a stage-2 capacity to regulate your immediate impulses and desires, a capacity that toddlers lack. Once this stage-2 capacity is gained, it is not lost as you move to higher stages. The capacity evident in the earlier stage is merely moved over from subject to object and is retained.

Before turning to a brief description of Kegan's stages 2 through 5, let's take a look at a few of the general features of Kegan's stage theory, as seen in the table on the next page. First, the subject/object distinction continues across all the stages. Whereas the stage-1 child is subject to her or his perceptions, impulses, and feelings, individuals at other stages are subject to (embedded in) other, increasingly more complicated perspectives. So even stage-3 adults (most adults appear to function at this stage), who have a more complex and encompassing view/experience of the world than children and most adolescents, are nonetheless embedded in or "subject to" a particular way of constructing reality. Although we may not yet have the capacity to see them, there may be more complex and encompassing ways of making sense of our experiences, ways that are as opaque to us as was the conservation of the amount of water in the two glasses to Piaget's four-year-old.

With the possible exception of individuals at Kegan's last stage, stage 5, each of us is ignorant about potentially more complete ways of constructing reality. Like Piaget's four-year-olds, we are probably embedded in a particular way of making sense of our experience. We don't know what we don't know, not because we lack experience, but because we lack a more complicated way of understanding what is being experienced. I think this is both disconcerting and exciting: disconcerting because it implies that there is a level of understanding that we lack, and exciting because it implies that no matter where we are in our life we will, with luck, become wiser.

STAGE/NAME	SUBJECT	OBJECT	PERSPECTIVE
1 (Impulsive)	Immediate perceptions, feelings, and impulses	Actions , sensa-tions and physical objects	Single perspective, can't take other's point of view
2 (Imperial)	Enduring interests, personal agendas, & role expectations	Immediate perceptions, feelings, and impulses	Can take multiple perspectives, one at a time
3 (Interpersonal)	Shared meaning, mutuality, social ideals & self - consciousness	Enduring interests, personal agendas, & role expectations	Can take two or more perspectives simultaneously
4 (Institutional)	A self-authored system of values and standards	Shared meaning, mutuality, social ideals & self - consciousness	Has own personal perspective on relationships and societal ideals
5 (Interindividual)	Universality, paradox, multiple "selves" as vehicles for connection	A self authored system of values and standards	Recognizes that own perspective on experience is a self-created convenience

Kegan's Stages of the Development of the Self (From Kegan, 1982, 1994)[8]

One somewhat troubling implication of this progressive, constructive/developmental view of how we make meaning is that understanding Kegan's higher stages may be beyond the conceptual capability of some readers. So, for example, if you are a stage-2 adult (it turns out there are quite a few out there), you will be unable to fully grasp Kegan's higher stages. Each stage is based on a progressively more complicated way of seeing the world. If you lack these more complicated perspectives, you are bound to simplify and misunderstand descriptions of what those higher stages are all about. And if you reassure yourself with the thought that you are probably pretty advanced in your thinking, you may find it sobering to learn that many first-time students of Kegan's theory tend to overestimate their developmental level. Remember, we have found that most adults are functioning at Kegan's stage 3, not stage 4. And very few individuals appear to be moving to Kegan's highest stage, stage 5. On the positive side, finding out that you may not be as highly evolved as you thought you were is valuable, because Kegan's theory can help you better understand where you are developmentally, and where you are headed. I hope you'll come to see that this can be a powerful kind of self-knowledge.

A second feature of the theory illustrated in the table is the way that what is "subject" at one stage becomes "object" at succeeding stages. So, for example, whereas perceptions are subject for the stage-1 preschooler, the school-age child (stage 2) has made those immediate perceptions the *object of* a new "subject." This is a pattern that is repeated each time one moves from one's current stage to the next stage. As Kegan puts it, development at each stage entails movement out of one embeddedness into another. But in the process, one can relate to and be "objective" about what one was formerly embedded in. Earlier ways of making sense of experience are not lost; they continue to be available to us to use or not use, depending on the circumstances. So, for example, even as adults we still have the capacity to maximize self-interest (self-interest is "subject" at stage 2), though most of the time we choose to control our self-interest by using one of the broader frames of reference we developed at stage 3 or beyond. Consider the following example. Imagine yourself approaching a red light at 5am. No one is around. You're in a hurry. So you drive through the red light ignoring your broader commitment to being a law-abiding citizen. You have acted as if you were a stage-2 person. You have "constructed" the situation in terms of your interest in hurrying to your destination; you thereby appear to be "subject to" your interests. But just because you drove through that red light doesn't mean your immediate interests define the upper limit of how you could have framed your situation at the intersection. Indeed, most of the time you probably choose to operate in terms of the more complicated perspectives of a higher stage (like thinking of yourself as a good citizen). In a similar vein, unlike the toddler described above, we're unlikely to scream "I hate you," when our boss refuses to give us the time off we need to go out of town to an interesting event. In fact, because of our greater capacity to hold together in our minds our boss's current refusal with her past generosity, we don't hate her at all. That's one way we've "grown up."

And finally, the table emphasizes how each stage is characterized by a particular level of social perspective-taking. The level of sophistication of these perspectives shapes our experience of reality. Kegan suggests that these perspective-taking capacities underlie the achievement of a broader and broader understanding of and connection to social reality at each successive stage. In Kegan's words,

> Subject-object relations emerge out of a lifelong process of development: a succession of qualitative differentiations of the self from the world, with a qualitatively more extensive object with which to be in relation created each time; a natural history of qualitatively better guarantees to the world of its distinctness; successive triumphs of "relationship to" rather than "embeddedness in."[9]

I invite you to reread that quote. It says something quite interesting about how the progressively more complex perspectives that we gain at successive developmental stages affect our experience of the world. At first you may have read the quote as saying that the person with a broader perspective understands more (the "more extensive object" phrase), a sort of "seeing the big picture" idea. But Kegan is actually saying something a good bit subtler and more interesting. This more interesting thing has to do with the "guarantee(ing) to the world its distinctness." This second idea is that only to the extent that we differentiate ourselves from "objects" in the world are we able to clearly see them for what they are. An interaction with my son comes to mind when I think about this phenomenon.

I'm a university professor who lives in a small town that is, in many ways, dominated by the university. Both of my children were aware from an early age that I teach at that university. I was struck, therefore, by the following question from my son, which came during his junior year in high school. I don't remember the actual context of his question, but I had a sense of it coming out of the blue. He asked, "Now, Dad, what is it that you actually do?" This may seem like an innocuous question to you, but I can assure you that it didn't feel that way to me. To me it felt like my son had just discovered me. It was as if he looked over at the bald, middle-aged guy reading the paper and wondered "who is this guy?" Something was happening to him that was enabling him to discern parts of me that had been there all along but that his "embeddedness" had prevented him from seeing. I know you may be thinking, "This guy needs to get a life," but I can tell you, it was downright exciting. "Wow," I remember feeling, "he really is going to grow up after all."

Why couldn't he "see" me prior to this point in time? The broad answer is that he was unable to see me, the university professor, because he was "embedded in" (or seeing me through the lens of) his interests and needs. Of course, he was already "seeing" me in one sense. But, as a stage-2 adolescent, he was seeing me in the context of his needs and interests. I was the guy who might lend him my car keys or might let him stay out with his friends. But the parts of me that existed independent of his needs, the university professor with a career, students, etc., barely existed in his need-centered, stage-2 world. Only as my son began to move his needs over from subject to object, to differentiate himself from his needs, did my existence as a person in my own right begin to take form. That was the sense in which I felt newly discovered, when he asked that seemingly innocuous question, ". . . what is it that you actually do?" You may be able to remember having that experience from the other side. When you began to think of and relate to your parents as people, not just your parents.

4 STAGE 2: LET'S MAKE A DEAL

The towering developmental achievement of stage 1 is the creation of a self that has its own perspective on the physical world and can distinguish itself from others, in a physical sense. But, at the same time, the stage-1 children are prisoners of their immediate experiences. Because the stage-1 child is embedded in ("subject to") her immediate experiences, she lacks the capacity to achieve a stable sense of self and a stable view of the world. So, for example, when your screaming toddler's feelings changed after supper, his experience of himself and of you also changed. This can be a chaotic way of living, and can be seen most dramatically in stage-1 adults, who are referred to by some clinicians as suffering from a "borderline personality disorder." The stage-1 individual, whether adult or child, suffers from a fundamental lack of emotional stability. It is precisely this instability that is reconstructed at stage 2. Beginning around age 5, the stage-1 child slowly develops a broader perspective within which to regulate his immediate perceptions, feelings, and impulses. In general terms, that broader perspective is one that endures across time and space. As a result, the child gains an enduring sense of self. He no longer *is* his immediate impulses and desires. Instead, he *has* impulses and desires, which he can regulate, using his new perspective-taking capacity. It is in this regard that Kegan suggests that stage 2 is the first developmental stage in which one gains a stable sense of self. No longer embedded in changing impulses, feelings, perceptions, and desires, stage 2 children (and adults) are instead identified with their *enduring* needs, interests and agendas. For the first time, the world becomes a stable place where psychological entities exist through time. Recall Antoine. He was aware that he had two competing desires: to bake cookies and to go to the store with his dad. At any given moment one or the other of the desires might have been dominant. But Antoine's developmental level (Kegan's stage 2) permitted him to "preserve" both desires in setting a priority or in negotiating with his parents to have both interests satisfied. Unlike little Jimmy, Antoine didn't loose one desire, when he pursued the other. Both endured and were psychologically preserved in Antoine's capacity to hold together multiple interests using a broader perspective.

Living through or organizing one's experiences through one's *enduring* needs and interests creates a particular kind of *intra*personal (internal) experience: the stage-2 person's stable sense of self. But moving to stage 2 also produces a transformation of the *inter*personal world, how one experiences others. The hallmark of Kegan's description of the stage-2 individual is her or his capacity to take multiple perspectives. Years ago, Piaget dramatically demonstrated how stage-1 children can see the world only from their own perspective. When asked to draw a picture of two different objects arranged from the child's left to right on a table between the child and Piaget, younger children simply drew what they saw - let's say a ball to the left, a box to the right. But when asked to draw these same two objects as seen by Piaget (who was on the other side of the table), Piaget's young children again drew it as it looked to them. In doing so, these stage-1 children demonstrated that they are embedded in and see the world through their own single perspective. What they see -- the ball to the left, the box to the right -- is what they think everyone sees. Similarly, stage-1 children assume that what they know, everyone knows. This is nicely illustrated when toddlers start telling you about something that just happened to them without bothering to telling you what they are referring to. If *they* know something, then they expect that *you* know it, too. So a toddler might approach you in tears from another room and say, "Tell Tommy to stop." This stage-1 toddler doesn't have the perspective-taking capacity to understand that you have no clue what he's talking about. This, by the way, is one reason that young children don't typically lie about what they have seen or done. It is only when a child has reached stage 2, where there is an understanding that different people can know different things, that lying becomes a psychological possibility. For example, if I realize that I ate a forbidden treat, and I know you don't know, then I can lie to you about it ("The dog ate it.") and, hopefully, not get into trouble. In contrast, your toddler thinks *you* know they ate the treat, because *they* know they ate it. You may want to remember this when one of your children tells her first lie. You are witnessing a momentous developmental change. She lied, she must be growing up!

Seeing the world from multiple perspectives imparts several capabilities that are essential to living effectively in what is a largely interpersonal world. One new capability is being able to take on fixed roles and to follow rules of behavior. Consider, for example, the practice of taking turns in elementary school. Most children, those who are "ready" for school, are able to understand and participate in the typical rule-bound elementary school classroom. In doing so, they are exercising their new-found ability to take another's (the teacher's) perspective. Personally, they may want to play with an attractive toy whenever they want or always be first in line for lunch. Instead, the stage-2 grade school child subjugates his immediate desires and follows the teacher's rule that says everyone must take turns. This ability to follow the rules is only possible, however, if the child can make her impulses object of a more enduring set of interests – perhaps an interest in being one of the teacher's favorites or being a "good girl." Stage-2 children acquire this ability to play by the rules -- to be "good" students, for example -- because they can see things from more perspectives than just their own. Kegan even suggests that this "birth of the role" is a cardinal feature of the transition from stage 1 to stage 2.[10]

You may have noticed that from time to time I have indicated that some adults are still functioning at stage 2. How might this look? Surely a stage-2 adult is not all about "being good" and "taking turns" the way an elementary school child is. Here's an excerpt from an assessment interview done with an 18-year-old college sophomore who my colleagues and I determined to be at stage 2.[11] The student is talking about another student, who unexpectedly confided in him about personal problems he was having.

> You know, we were tight as friends. But I was still kind of surprised that he would trust me enough to do that. You know, for him to think that highly of me to tell me something like that. You know I wouldn't want to stab this person in the back. If I can, I'd like to help him out. If he's having some trouble and I can help him get out of that, I want to. Trust is important in relationships. I've seen people say one thing and their action is totally different. And after a while you can't trust them because after a while you're like "Oh, he's lying again." He lied before and he'll lie again. And if I lose him as a friend, then I can't be learning anything from him.

Here we have a young adult, a college sophomore, who demonstrates at least two socially acceptable characteristics. He wants to help a friend who is having personal problems. And he thinks relationships have to be based on trust. "Wait a minute," you may be thinking, "I share those views." "Does that mean I'm also stage 2?" Probably not. Let's look at what the "deep structure" of these remarks is. First, this student is able to see things from more than one perspective. He understands that the friend's problems are not his own problems. And he also understands that people can lie to one another. So he is able to take multiple (in this case two) perspectives. And so can you. But if you are beyond stage 2, then you will be able to do *more* than construct your understanding of friendships in terms of two *alternative* perspectives. Notice that this student is concerned about lying in a relationship because it can lead to losing that person as a friend. And what's bad about that is not that a special bond has been broken. What's bad is that the student will lose something that he, personally, is interested in -- learning something valuable from the friend (look at his last statement). In short, friends are valuable because you get something you want out of the relationship. Lying makes it impossible to predict what your friend will do. So if your friend lies, you can't rely on him for help. Missing in this short excerpt is a stage-3 understanding of relationships as a *shared* psychological experience, the joint internal experience of knowing that you each care about the experience that the other has of you. Instead, for this student, relationships are valuable for at least two reasons that have nothing to do with a shared feeling or bond. For this student, a friendship is the setting in which he can meet his individual goal of helping others. Trust is valuable to him, because it means that his friends will help him out when he needs it. What our student wants is to be able to help others and he wants to be able to count on others' help when he needs it. In short, he is subject to both of these personal interests (see the description of stage 2 in the table back on page 36).

You may at this point be thinking that this distinction between a stage-2 and a stage-3 view of relationships is pretty subtle.

In fact, it isn't at all subtle. This distinction is merely hard to recognize until you train yourself to look for the "deep structure" behind a person's words. The differences between stage-2 and stage-3 individuals are profound, as you will see more clearly when we move to a description of stage 3 in the next chapter. What is "subtle" or difficult is distinguishing the *content* of a person's utterances and actions from the *underlying capacities* or *structures* that are generating those utterances. At this point, you may have to accept on faith that the student described above is functioning at Kegan's stage 2. But you should take note of the fact that, like this student, stage-2 individuals can be "good" people with socially acceptable motives. Just because individuals are subject to their interests and agendas, they aren't necessarily selfish or only "looking out for number one."

In his 1994 book Kegan offers an expanded description of the underlying structure of stage-2 meaning-making.[12] Recall again the older child in Piaget's beaker experiment. It was suggested that this child mentally "conserved" the liquid in the two beakers by "reasoning about" his perceptions. Little was said, however, about what that reasoning process consisted of. In his 1994 book, Kegan provides an answer that pertains to views of the self and of others, as well as the properties of objects. The stage-2 child (in contrast to the stage-1 child) has discovered that objects, including the self and other people, have "durable properties."[13] So for Piaget's older child, the water in the beakers has the durable quality of volume.

Even if it looks like there's more liquid, there isn't. But the stage-2 individual also does a similar sort of conserving with respect to the self and others. Now, just like the liquid in the beaker, the *self* is viewed as having durable qualities. One such durable quality in the student described above is his commitment to helping out his friends. This interest is durable because it's not based on how he's feeling at the moment. Arguably, even when he doesn't feel like helping out a friend, he may well override his immediate feelings and help. In short, wanting to help others is one of his "durable" qualities. This is another way of understanding how a stage-2 individual is said to have a stable sense of self that a stage-1 individual lacks. At stage 2 there's a larger *me* that has durable, continuing qualities. The same reasoning process can be applied to the stage-2 individual's experience of other people. Recall the toddler's temper tantrum ("I hate you."). This stage-1 child experiences daddy through her or his immediate feelings and desires. When the toddler was hating daddy, daddy *was* hateful. In contrast, the stage-2 child understands that daddy has durable characteristics. He knows that "daddy loves me," even as he is hating him. His immediate experience of his father doesn't alter his perception of his father's inner (durable) qualities. For the stage-2 child, "me hating daddy" is quite separate from "daddy loving me." Daddy is seen as having his own enduring interests and intentions. In 1994 Kegan called this fundamental stage-2 capacity the "principle of durable categories" and it compliments his view that stage-2 individuals can take multiple perspectives one at a time.

A comment is in order here about Kegan's 1982 name for stage 2: the "imperial stage." It is relatively easy to see why Kegan called stage 1 the "impulsive" stage. The stage-1 child is subject to/embedded in his impulses (see the Table on page 36). But in what way is the stage-2 individual "imperial?" The answer is that even though the stage-2 individual has the capacity to see things from another's point of view, his or her own enduring interests and agendas are paramount. The stage-2 person's whole sense of self is tied up in being able to be effective in achieving valued objectives. This view is consistent with Erik Erikson's focus on the centrality of "competence" during this pre-adolescent developmental period. One's sense of competence is dependent upon being able to achieve one's goals. There's an apocryphal story that illustrates this "imperial" quality of the stage-2 pre-adolescent. Spotting an elderly woman standing at the intersection of a busy city street with several large packages at her feet, the eager young Boy Scout rushes to her aid. He snatches up her packages and escorts her across the street by her arm. Safely on the other side she turns to him and remarks, "Thank you young man, but I was waiting over there for someone to pick me up." Arguably, this stage-2 Boy Scout was helping this elderly woman because *he* had an interest in being helpful, not because she needed his help. The apparently needy woman became important to the Boy Scout, because she provided an opportunity for him to be a competent helper. In his inability to construct a shared understanding of the encounter, he was being Kegan's stage-2 “imperial” self.

While stage-2 perspective-taking is a highly significant improvement over the very limited perspective taking of the stage-1 child, it is ordinarily not sufficient for effective functioning in the adult world. As adults, we are more than a little annoyed by people who imperially manipulate us to get what they want. And we don’t appreciate it when we are involved in a friendship with a person who seems always to be keeping a running tally of who has done more favors for the other. Stage-2 teenagers and adults don’t seem to understand that relationships can be more than an alliance in which each party to the relationship gets something they desire or value from the other. It’s not that we reject the notion of fairness or balanced contributions in relationships. What bothers us the most is that the stage-2 person seems to think that fairness and equal exchange is the *only* thing that relationships are about. In contrast to our teenagers’ and stage-2 friends’ views, most of us believe a more important feature of relationships is a kind of *shared internal experience*, how we feel about how each other. In Kegan’s theory this sort of shared interpersonal experience is a function of being able to construct one’s experience of one’s relationships using a stage-3 perspective. It’s not that stage-2 individuals don’t *value* shared experiences. They simply don’t have them.

5 STAGE 3 – CREATING AN INTERPERSONAL SELF

For the person functioning at Kegan's stage 2, relationships entail the coordination of two sets of needs: what one person desires and what the other person desires. There is a clear recognition of the other person as a separate individual with his or her own separate needs and interests. But in a fundamental way, the stage-2 person's experience of his partner remains an external experience. What others think and feel may matter to him, but it doesn't become a feature of the stage-2 individual's sense of self. The monumental shift in perspective-taking that occurs with the advent of stage 3 is the capacity to make another's experience of us *a part of* our own experience of ourselves. The stage-3 "deep structure" that creates this new understanding of relationships is being able to take two social perspectives *simultaneously*. We often see the first expressions of this capacity in early adolescence. Consider the following. My13-year-old daughter left for school one morning in apparent good humor. A few minutes later I was surprised to hear her returning through the front door. Going to see what brought her back, I discovered her in tears. Thinking she'd probably had another encounter with the neighborhood bully, I asked her what was wrong. Her reply was, "Everybody's going to think my shoes look stupid." My first impulse was to try to reassure her that her shoes looked fine and that nobody would notice. Instead, struck by the emerging developmental change that this small incident reflected, I told my daughter to change her shoes and that I'd drive her back to school. What caught my attention was that this was the first time that I saw her making what she thought someone might be thinking about her a part of the way she thought about himself. Of course, I could have been wrong about this. It's possible that this was still just a stage-2 concern. Stage-2 children, after all, do care about what others think about them. But the reason they care is that they are worried that if others don't like them, then the others won't want to do fun things with them, or worse, will tease them. In other words, what other children think about a child functioning at stage 2 is important *external* information for predicting how others are going to behave. But notice that for the stage-2 child, others' views of him are located "out there" in the heads of those others. The fundamental shift in conceptual capacity from stage 2 to stage 3 is the gaining of the ability to take an external view of oneself ("They'll think I look stupid") and make it a part of the internal experience of oneself ("I feel stupid").

You may remember from Chapter 2 that I used another example of how stage-2 and stage-3 meaning-making differ. That was the example of the couple where each, occasionally, failed to show up on time. I suggested that their very different experiences of being kept waiting by the other could be a function of their being at two different developmental stages. In the example, I suggested that you (as a person functioning at stage 3) were oriented to how your friend's being late might reflect an unfavorable change in what he *thought about* you. You worried, for example, that his being late could mean you were being "taken for granted." He, on the other hand (depicted as being at stage 2), was concerned about how your being late interfered with what he wanted to do. He became angry, and he showed no apparent concern over how his anger might make you feel. Instead, his anger was a result of your inconveniencing him and a way of clearly indicating to you how he wanted you to behave in the future. This example illustrates how stage-2 individuals are primarily interested in predicting and controlling the *outcomes* of interactions, while stage-3 individuals are primarily concerned about the quality of their internal experiences of others' experiences of them. This can be seen by considering another example.

A female electrical engineer attending a professional meeting in a city far from home is approached at a cocktail party by a very attractive man who suggests that she accompany him to his room for a drink. She's pretty sure where this will lead. Her husband, a social worker, never attends these yearly meetings and has very little contact with engineers. It's highly unlikely, therefore, that he would ever find out what has happened in a hotel room twenty-five hundred miles from home. Our engineer has to make a decision. Will she go up to the room with this attractive man, or will she turn him down? Let's see how a stage-2 individual might think about this proposition. She would, first and foremost, be concerned about potential negative consequences to herself. She loves her husband (in a stage-2 manner) and values the things she gains from her marriage. So she's not going to do anything to threaten her marriage. But she also realizes that it is extremely unlikely that her husband will ever find out. And this guy is *very* appealing. She heads up to his room. We next see her getting off the plane back home. Her husband is there to meet her, and he rushes up and throws his arms around her telling her how much he missed her. How does she feel? If you thought "guilty," you'd be wrong. What she, as a stage-2 person, is more likely to be feeling than guilt is *worry*, worry that however unlikely it is, her husband might somehow find out that she was unfaithful to him. And seeing him again only reminds her how much she values their marriage and how much she hopes he never does find out.

Now imagine the same situation with our electrical engineer, but imagine that she makes sense of her experiences using a stage-3, not a stage-2 capacity. Facing the same decision at the cocktail party, she, too, thinks about her husband. Her husband is twenty-five hundred miles away blissfully unaware of her temptation. But because she constructs meaning using a stage-3 frame, she has a very different experience as she thinks about her husband than did our stage-2 engineer. In a psychological sense, the husband of our stage-3 engineer is right there with her *in her head*. Her sense of self, her very identity, is constructed out of an *inner* sense of her loving her husband loving her. They have a shared love that is at the very heart of her sense of who she is. It doesn't matter that her husband is *physically* thousands of miles away. *Psychologically* he's right there in her head (and heart); he's a part of the way in which she experiences herself. But let's assume that she's had way too much to drink and has lost her capacity to think clearly. She accepts this stranger's offer of a drink and heads off to his hotel room. Again, we next see her getting off the plane upon her arrival home. As her husband throws his arms around her and tells her how much he missed her, what does she feel? This time if you thought "guilt," you'd be correct! It doesn't matter that he will probably never find out about her liaison at the convention hotel. Even if he never finds out, she has compromised her *own* sense of shared trust by being unfaithful to her husband. She can no longer feel reassured by the knowledge that her husband trusts her, because she thinks that if he knew what she did, his trust in her would be severely weakened. After all, how does it feel to be trusted when you know you haven't been trustworthy? Arguably, her distress is evidence of what we understand to be a "guilty conscience." Like many other developmental phenomena, this capability to experience a guilty conscience or true guilt (as opposed to the stage-2 person's "worry") is both a developmental achievement and, at times, a burden. The pleasure she used to take in experiencing herself being loved and trusted by him now rings hollow. Because stage-3 individuals carry around their relationships inside their own heads in this way, it is probably safe to say that stage-3 individuals are less likely to cheat on their spouses than are stage-2 individuals. But not always. A stage-2 person who has a strong personal interest in being faithful to her husband might well resist the temptation to stray from her marital vows, because she is embedded in her *enduring interest* in remaining faithful to her husband (remember, one's enduring, individual interests are "subject" at stage 2 – you may want to look back at that table in Chapter 3). This is why it's important to distinguish between how individuals structure their experience versus how they behave. Kegan's vision is, after all, a *cognitive* theory of personality, not a behavioral theory. In the above example we considered how our engineer would think and feel about her temptation, no matter what she ended up actually doing.

This analysis of our female engineer also helps illuminate the issue of jealousy. Why is it, you may have wondered, that some people tend toward jealousy and distrust in close relationships while others are unfailingly trusting? Common wisdom suggests that the origin of jealousy is low self-esteem. An alternative possibility is that jealousy and distrust are stage-2 phenomena. Stage-2 individuals, lacking the capacity to internalize another's caring for them, need to have that caring demonstrated over and over again in very concrete ways. And lacking an internal presence of the other's caring as a part of their ongoing sense of self (an experience that requires stage-3 simultaneous perspective-taking), the stage-2 person believes that it is tempting to cheat on one's partner, if there will be no negative external consequences. For the stage-3 individual, the consequences of cheating on someone whom you love are, first and foremost, internal, and therefore, inescapable. In this way, if we are at stage 3, there are always negative consequences for cheating (they are internal), so we are less likely to think jealously that our lover (whom we tend to believe thinks and feels the same stage-3 manner that we do) could be cheating on us.

Above I made a distinction between true guilt and a "guilt" that is actually a kind of worry. The former requires a stage-3 way of constructing experience, the latter only stage 2. Let's look at the dynamics of stage-3 guilt a little more closely. Let's say you know that your mother is going to be upset that you forgot to send her a birthday card. You feel guilty. And you imagine that she's going to get her feelings hurt. As someone functioning at stage 3, you make her experience of your forgetting her birthday a part of your own experience of yourself. It makes you feel bad just knowing that she thinks you've forgotten about her. You imagine that *her* sense of self has also been compromised, because she thinks you must not care as much about her as she thought you did. And because we often think those we love construct meaning in the same way we do, we believe our mother makes the idea that we don't care as much as we used to an internal part of her sense of herself. Hence the familiar phrase, "I hurt her feelings." Feeling guilty is possible for you, but not for your stage-2 siblings or friends, because you have the stage-3 capacity to create shared or simultaneous perspectives and because you imagine (whether it's true or not) that your mother has that same capacity. So, much as you may dislike feeling guilty, feeling guilty is in fact a developmental achievement.

Despite the fact that achieving stage-3 perspective-taking brings with it the sometimes painful experience of "true" guilt, there are, of course, many positives associated with reaching stage 3. Indeed, guilt can be a very effective motivator for doing the right thing. For example, most employers want their employees to feel bad if they don't do a good job, even if the employer may never find out. Arguably, stage-2 employees, unable to internalize their employer's view of them, will slack off, if there are no negative consequences for doing so, and if working hard is not one of the stage-2 employee's individual interests. Stage-3 employees are less likely to slack off, because they are embedded in the *internal experience of* how their supervisors think about them. And they like the internal experience of thinking about themselves as the kind of person that cares about their work. Either way, they feel guilty if they don't meet what are, in effect, internalized shared expectations. As a result, stage-3 employees don't require the level of direct supervision that stage-2 employees often do.

The example of the female engineer at her professional meeting suggests another positive achievement associated with progressing to stage 3. Since stage-3 individuals are able to carry their relationships around with them in their heads, they have an ongoing sense of shared meaning, shared security, and shared loyalty to their relationships. A stage-3 individual can console herself with the thought "I know we'll always have a special bond," or "He sometimes gets too caught up in his work, but I know he really loves me." At stage 2 you have to be sure that you are meeting your partner's needs so that they will continue to meet yours. At stage 3 that pressure to perform, to meet the other's needs, is greatly reduced. To a large extent, stage-3 individuals sustain relationships merely by letting each other know how they *feel* about one another. In Kegan's words,

> (achieving stage 3) "...frees one of having to exercise so much control over an otherwise unfathomable world. It frees me from the distrust of a world from which (at stage 2) I am radically separate. Without the internalization of the other's voice in one's very construction of self, how one feels (at stage 2) is much more a matter of how external others will react, and the universal effort to preserve one's integrity will be felt by others as an effort to control and manipulate" (material in parentheses added for clarity)[14].

You can see this if you reconsider the example of the forgotten birthday, where the actor is stage 2, not stage 3. Forgetting his mother's birthday, the stage-2 individual still might say that he "feels guilty," because he's heard others use that phrase in similar circumstances. But what he really experiences is not what most of us consider to be guilt. Instead, what he probably feels is worry about what his mother may withhold from him as a result of his thoughtlessness. The next time he needs a little cash, he wonders, can he count on her?

In his 1982 description of his theory, Kegan termed stage 3

the "interpersonal" stage. You probably have a feel for why Kegan selected this name. Stage-3 individuals are "interpersonal" in a way that stage-1 and stage-2 individuals are not. Stage 3 people alone are "subject to" their shared, interpersonal experiences. At least during the early years of functioning at stage 3, they experience the world primarily in terms of shared interpersonal connections. But to call stage 3 "interpersonal" is somewhat restricted, because it fails to capture two additional aspects of stage-3 experience that lie outside a narrow definition of the term "interpersonal" (in fact, Kegan dropped this label in his 1994 book). These are social *idealism* and psychological *subjectivity*. Let's start with idealism. Children are not idealistic. Idealism doesn't usually emerge until one has reached chronological adolescence. Many teenagers (but not all of them -- remember, some people are slow getting past stage 2) embrace lofty ideals, like conserving the planet's precious natural resources, or working for social justice, and they find fault with adults for not adopting lifestyles that are consistent with the ideals they hear adults espousing. They are, in short, being "idealistic." But what has happened to make teenagers this way? Have they merely learned more about the world and how broken and fragile it is? In other words, is *amount* of knowledge a satisfactory explanation of the emergence of adolescent idealism? Kegan thinks not. Idealism, in Kegan's theory, is another expression of stage 3 *structural* capacity. True, the adolescent must acquire certain knowledge about how fragile the planet is to care about global resources. But just that knowledge alone, what is considered "content knowledge" in

Kegan's theory, is insufficient without the capacity to "structure" or organize that knowledge in an idealistic fashion. Kegan's view is that idealism (just like interpersonalism) requires the capacity to take two perspectives simultaneously. What makes idealism seem different from interpersonalism is that in idealism the other perspective that is being internalized by the stage-3 adolescent is not an *individual's* perspective. Instead it is a generalized or *societal* perspective.

When an adolescent adopts a societal perspective as her own (note: there are two perspectives here - the societal ideal and what the adolescent believes), she is *co-constructing* her identity as someone who cares about the planet, just as surely as she has co-constructed her identity with a close friend's experience of her. Only now she's not so much concerned with maintaining her close friend's positive view of her as she is with maintaining society's positive view of her. But notice that in both instances (what she thinks her friend thinks about her, and what she thinks society expects or thinks of her), her concern grows out of a stage-3 structural capacity to take two perspectives simultaneously. In contrast to stage-2 meaning-making, stage-3 idealism is not about satisfying one's own enduring needs and interests or meeting certain simple role expectations. Instead, idealism is about subordinating self-interest to something larger than the self. That "something larger" is a shared perspective (for example, the idealist is a *part of* a larger community committed to conserving the earth's natural resources). At Kegan's stage 3, one's idealism co-defines the self. Notice that I said "co-defines" the self. That "co-" is important. Without it we have a more advanced "ideology" that is the individual's alone. This sort of self-determined ideology is the hallmark of Kegan's stage 4. I'll say more about this in the chapter describing Kegan's stage 4.

Idealism often seems like a developmental advance over interpersonalism. (For those of you familiar with the work of Lawrence Kohlberg, you may remember that Kohlberg does, indeed, divide these two sensibilities into two adjacent stages of moral decision-making.[15]) But Kegan put both interpersonalism and idealism into the *same* stage, stage 3, because he believes they share the same "deep structure" -- the capacity to take two perspectives simultaneously. What sometimes makes Kegan's position on this issue less than fully satisfying to me is that one's ideals can appear to relativize or seem to make "object" one's relationships. So, for example, I have heard students remark, "I don't care what others think of me, as long as I'm being a good Christian." This sure sounds to me as if the student has moved past a narrow interpersonal embeddedness. But because the two types of identity do indeed share the same underlying organizing principle (simultaneous perspective taking), Kegan puts them both in stage 3. And I suppose that's where they both belong. But I still believe that it is worth noting that "idealistic" stage-3 individuals behave and, at least on the surface, appear to think more broadly than do "interpersonal" stage-3 individuals. Nonetheless, as you'll discover in the next chapter, stage-3 idealism is not the same as self-authored stage-4 ideology. Stage-4 individuals think things through for themselves; stage-3 "idealists" make sure that what they think is consistent with what those "in the know" think. Sometimes it is devilishly hard to sort this out, particularly if you can't directly question the person whose meaning-making stage is in question.

There are, fortunately, some clues that can help. One tip-off is that stage-3 idealists are convinced that others who don't share their views are not merely holders of different views: they're wrong. So, for example, while both stage-3 and stage-4 parents may think their daughter made a terrible mistake when she decided to major in psychology or English instead of business, only the stage-3 parents feel like a failure as a result. There's a kind of dogmatic certainty lurking here. According to Kegan, the dynamics of this sort of dogmatism stem from the fact that idealistic (stage-3) individuals are embedded in or personally identified with the societal views that they hold (or more accurately "the ideals they are held by"). For them, any shared view (e.g., people in the know say students should major in a "practical" field) is "subject." To abandon or abdicate that view amounts, in a psychological sense, to an abandonment or abdication of a part of oneself (if *I* believe it, then I have to ensure that my children live it). Only after reaching Kegan's stage 4 are people able to take as a given that others may construct valid alternative value-systems based on their unique life experiences. As you'll see below, stage-4 individuals can grant a freedom of personal choice to others, because they have granted it to themselves. In short, when a stage-4 perspective-taking capacity emerges, then the dogmatism and idealistic certainty of stage 3 subside.[16]

"Wait just a minute," you may be saying. "I know lots of seemingly stage-3 people who value diversity and tolerance of differences. Now you're saying that only after arriving at stage 4 can someone truly respect others' differences." The constructive/developmental take on this very good observation is that in our society people are often told they *should* value diversity and be tolerant of others' differences. And wanting to be good citizens, they try to make these societal expectations a part of themselves. But that doesn't mean they have "internalized" these principles. If the upper limit of their perspective-taking capacity is Kegan's stage 3, they will connect to or co-construct themselves with the societal view that tolerance and diversity are good things to believe. And they will advocate these ideas and try to live lives consistent with them. But in a fundamental way, they won't be able to enact these values in the absence of continuing societal support. Witness the way Americans initially responded to the Patriot Act's abridgement of individual freedoms. Most Americans, when given a good rationale for the Act's abridgements, particularly when the rationale was provided by credible people (like George W. Bush in 2002), had little difficulty moving to another position where national security and holding fast against terrorists became the paramount value, not individual freedom. What happened to tolerance and freedom? Well, maybe for a lot of people it wasn't a *personal* value in the first place. Instead it was, for many people, a shared (read "stage-3") value. And if the part of society you share that value with starts singing a different tune, you start singing along. You can undoubtedly think of many other recent examples where large segments of society quickly "abandoned" cherished values in the face of some sort of crisis. But "abandoned" is probably the wrong word for describing what happened. More likely, the prevailing societal view shifted, and stage-3 idealists who are, as Kegan puts it, "shared by" society, were swept along with the shift. In sum, idealism emerges for the first time as a feature of the stage-3 capacity to create a shared or collective identity. But as a "shared" identity it has certain limitations that are only overcome when one moves to stage 4.

6 STAGE 3 THOUGHT ALSO CREATES A NEW KID OF SUBJECTIVE EXPERIENCE

The other major feature of Kegan's stage 3 that is not well described by labeling stage 3 as "interpersonalism" is what Kegan terms the emergence of "int*ra*personal subjectivity." Becoming stage 3 not only fundamentally alters one's relationship to others and to society. When one gains the capacity for simultaneous perspective-taking (the hallmark of stage 3), one also gains a new kind of *inner* experience of the self as well. Stage-3 individuals are able to reflect upon themselves in a manner that creates one's first real *psychological* identity. To use an old term from the psychotherapy field, stage-3 individuals are "psychologically minded," while stage-2 individuals are not. What does this mean? Kegan presents the following two examples. When asked, "How would you describe yourself?" one child responded as follows:

> Brownish, I mean blondish brown hair. Blue eyes. I'm medium in height. My favorite computer game is Atari. I have a little sister. I'm mad at her. I'm smart. I'm *very* smart and I color neat. I like BLT sandwiches. I like everybody who likes me. Especially my best friend Robbi. She's super nice to me. [17]

Another child responded as follows:

> I'm becoming, like, much more confident. I used to be just super insecure and stuff, very self-conscious, and now I like myself

> much better and I think other people, like, are more comfortable with me, and like me better too, y'know what I mean?[18]

You will not be surprised to learn that the first quote is from a stage-2 eight-year-old, the second quote from a stage-3 teenager. Notice that what the younger child reflects upon are fixed characteristics, in the sense that they are manifestly present as she describes them. Some are "external," like her physical attributes. Others are "internal," like her being mad at her little sister and liking her best friend, Robbi. In contrast, the personal characteristics that the stage-3 adolescent reflects upon are more abstract. They can be understood to be generalizations about the sorts of simple inner characteristics the younger child describes. Experiences like "self-conscious" and "insecure" suggest that the stage-3 speaker is generalizing about *multiple* internal states and feelings. As Kegan suggests, these are "feelings about feelings" and as such demonstrate the stage-3 individual's capacity for the psychological experience of "subjectivity" or "psychological mindedness." This difference in the complexity of self-reflection between stage-2 and stage-3 individuals is one reason that some teenagers, when they experience the stage-2 to stage-3 transition, become dramatically more moody and sensitive than they were in the past. From the perspective of Kegan's theory, teen-aged moodiness probably has less to do with "raging hormones" than with teenagers' emerging capacity for self-reflection.

The above contrast between a stage-2 eight-year-old and a stage-3 teenager is easy to see, in part because of their age differences. But how might a stage-2 *teenager* describe himself? He's not likely to say the same kinds of things about himself that our eight-year-old did. Kegan doesn't present any examples of how a stage-2 adolescent would respond to an invitation to describe him or herself. But here's an example from my own research: a brief excerpt of a stage-2 college student describing his reaction to having earned a good grade.

> My goal was to improve over what I got last time. That was my goal, and I felt a lot better about myself, I guess, knowing that I reached it. I felt great. I mean I finally got an A on it. So I had gone above what I wanted to do, and so I was satisfied. I felt great.

As with the eight-year-old, this stage-2 teenager is expressing his feelings. But his feelings are not feelings about feelings. He is merely reporting on how he feels about having met an important goal. He shows no capacity to reflect upon his feelings of satisfaction. So, for example, he doesn't say, "I guess I have a pretty intense need for achievement." He doesn't demonstrate a capacity to reflect upon the issue of what kind of a person he has become as a result of being successful. As the rest of the interview demonstrated (not reported here) this level of self-reflection was noticeably absent in this stage-2 student.

The lack of a more "psychological" level of self-reflection in stage-2 individuals has implications for our understanding of psychological problems. For years in the fields of child psychiatry and child clinical psychology, there has been a debate over whether pre-teenaged children could become depressed. It turns out that the question was not a good one, as it focused on the child's age instead of the child's developmental level. Kegan's theory allows us to consider this question in a more fruitful fashion. Kegan's theory suggests that stage-3 teenagers (and adults), with their greater capacity for self-reflection, become depressed *in a different way* than do stage-2 children (and stage-2 adults). For the more psychologically advanced teenagers (those at stage 3), depression is a fundamentally *internal* experience and more like what clinicians typically mean when they say someone is depressed. For the psychologically less developed stage-2 adolescent, the experience is more *external*. What do I mean in saying this? Imagine that Kegan's 8-year-old's friend, Robbi, moved away. This might be "depressing" in a way, but it would not likely evoke the painful internal self recrimination that we often see in depressed adults. Likewise, the stage-2 college student quoted above might become "depressed," if his grades fell. But he would be unable to become worried over what sort of a person this signaled he had become. This sort of internal focus would require stage-3 reflectiveness, something that is lacking in individuals functioning at stage 2. This is just one example of how a good theory of normal personality development might improve our understanding of psychopathology. Arguably, knowing someone's developmental level is central to understanding fully the dynamics of that person's psychological experiences.

Let's consider one more example of the difference between stage-2 and stage-3 subjective feelings. It is not uncommon to hear or recall conversations that go something like this: "Do you really love me? Sometimes I get the idea that you don't love me as much as I love you." Looking a bit surprised (or annoyed, if he's heard all this before), he answers, "Of course I love you. Do you think I'd still be here, if I didn't love you? Look at all the things I do for you. Don't you enjoy being with me? You know you do; and I love being with you and all the fun we have together. Of course I love you." But she seems oddly unconvinced and struggles on. "Well, it's just that sometimes I feel like you don't really share your true feelings with me, how you feel *inside* about me. It's almost as if how I feel about you doesn't matter as much to you as I once thought it did." And so it goes, and ultimately this conversation doesn't end up with her feeling she knows much more about how he *really* feels about her.

Do you see what's going on here? She's stage 3, so her subjective inner experiences are a whole lot more complex than his are. She has feelings about her feelings and thoughts about her thoughts. He has feelings and thoughts. She shares what it feels like to be loved by someone loving her. He shares what it feels like to enjoy doing things with her and for her. And because she hasn't read this book, she thinks he's holding back from her the kind of stuff she shares with him. But he's not. He's being as forthright as she is. But his inner world is a lot simpler and more one-dimensional than her inner world. This may be why she sometime feels emotionally closer to her girlfriends than she does to her husband or boyfriend. It also explains why she is wrong when she wonders if men and women are just different in how they share their feelings with one another. In this instance, it's not a gender difference; it's a developmental difference.

One of the attractions of Kegan's theory is its scope. The theory addresses a broad spectrum of psychological phenomena. Here's another example: consider Kegan's view of the structural determinants of what is known as "adolescent impulsivity." One of the perplexing characteristics of early adolescence is the adolescent's failure, in the heat of the moment, to consider the potential long-term consequences of his or her behavior. So, for example, many adolescents engage in unprotected sexual intercourse, despite knowing that they could contract AIDS or other sexually transmitted diseases. Others invest little effort in their schoolwork, despite knowing that they will need to have good grades to have any chance of getting admitted to their favorite college. The perplexing thing about these adolescents' risky and irresponsible behaviors is that they are typically fully aware of the future consequences of their current behaviors. They know they should use contraceptives to avoid contracting AIDS. They want to have good grades so they can get into the college of their choice. But caring about and knowing these things often seems to have little or no impact on their ongoing behavior. Why is this so? If you ask most developmental psychologists this question, they will typically invoke a concept labeled "adolescent invulnerability."[19] In their view, adolescents know about bad outcomes, but they don't think that they, personally, will experience those outcomes. Hence the term "adolescent invulnerability." But is this really an adequate explanation? Do we actually believe, for example, that our adolescent son doesn't think he will be hurt by bad grades?

Kegan has an entirely different take on the adolescent's "impulsivity." Kegan suggests that anticipating the future is dependent upon the development of a stage-3 way of making sense of one's experience. Stage-2 adolescents simply lack the structural capacity needed to be directly affected by future consequences. From Kegan's perspective, anticipating the future entails more than knowing and caring about what the long-term consequences of one's behavior may be. In Kegan's view, in order to be able to act responsibly one must make one's possible future *a part of* one's *present* experience. This entails having the stage-3 capacity to hold two perspectives (what I want now and what I want in the future) together at the *same time*. Stage-2 individuals can't do this. Instead, they have two separate sets of interests: what they want to accomplish in the present, and what they want to accomplish/avoid in the future. In other words, stage-2 adolescents have both sets of interests, but they have them *one at a time*. And sometimes these are *competing* interests (e.g. playing a video game or studying for tomorrow's test). In the heat of the moment, when the stage-2 adolescent is engaged by a present interest (e.g., "I want to play Halo with my friends,") rather than some future interest ("I want to get good grades"), the present interest triumphs. Of course, they're in better shape than their stage-1 counterparts, because unlike their younger counterparts, they can use their long-term interests to subordinate and control their immediate impulses (see the Table in chapter 3). So when we accuse teenagers of having poor impulse control, we are not being accurate. Instead, what they actually lack is one type of "common sense," where common sense is a product of the capacity to make one's future *a part of* one's present. In other words, Kegan suggests, so-called adolescent impulsivity is a product of the stage-2 adolescent's inability to hold two perspectives together at the same time. Being clear about the nature of the adolescent's deficiency can make a difference. If we, as parents, think our adolescents are suffering from adolescent invulnerability, then we do our best to convince them that they are, indeed, at risk. If, on the other hand, we recognize that our adolescent lacks a certain developmental capacity, the capacity to hold together internally present and future interests, then we need to provide the coordination of these two perspectives that our adolescent can't yet provide for himself. You may think the following is a trivial suggestion, but how about mounting a small picture of his favorite college on top of his video monitor? See if that's more effective than constantly reminding him that he's not going to get into a "good" college, if he doesn't study. The former strategy is an attempt to make his future goal salient while he is sitting down at his computer to play a video game or edit his Facebook files. The latter strategy is aimed at reminding him that he's not invulnerable to the usual consequences of not studying. It seems to me that those of us who are interested in helping our stage-2 children become more successful need to try to figure out ways to keep their own future goals and interests present in their minds, when their minds are on more exciting activities. Perhaps this is part of the success of a sexual abstinence program I recall reading about where at-risk teenage girls not only publicly pledged to wait until marriage before engaging in sexual intercourse but also wore wedding rings to remind themselves of that pledge.

What distinguishes the stage-3 adolescent from the stage-2 adolescent is the stage-3 adolescent's ability to think about, and thus coordinate in time, multiple sets of interests. In the structural terms of Kegan's theory, interests have been moved over from being "subject" at stage 2 to being "object" at stage 3. The stage-3 teenager connects her future with her present through her use of a perspective that encompasses both. In being able to make the future alive in the present, the stage-3 adolescent becomes "responsible" in a way that the stage-2 adolescent is not yet able to be. Those of us who try to parent adolescents hope that this key developmental transition occurs before our adolescents make bone-headed decisions that may significantly restrict their future opportunities. For that reason, parents who study Kegan's theory always want to know if they can accelerate the transition from stage-2 to stage-3 thinking in their children. Probably, but a summary of how Kegan proposes this can be accomplished will have to wait until we take up the issue of the dynamics of developmental change in chapter 9. Suffice it to say that, in an important way, successful parenting should include helping children develop increasingly complex ways of understanding their increasingly complex worlds.

The Limitations of Stage 3. Stage 3 is, without a doubt, a towering developmental achievement. It imparts the capacity for true interpersonal mutuality and the capacity to embrace ideals that transcend narrow self-interest. Interpersonal awareness and sensitivity increase as does the capacity to reflect upon one's own psychological characteristics (i.e., psychological mindedness). Merely sharing one's feelings with a person one cares about becomes a highly satisfying end in itself. Stage-3 functioning is very common. Nearly half of all adults in Western societies appear to spend most of their chronological adulthood making sense of their lives using Kegan's stage 3 or struggling to make the transition from stage 3 to stage 4.[20] Those adults who have not progressed to stage 3 may find it difficult to participate fully in many areas of adult life, from work to intimate relationships, areas of life that are managed relatively easily by those at stage 3. Still, stage 3 is not the last stage of the development of the self as envisioned by Kegan. It is not even the next to the last. It has substantial limitations with respect to living fully in a complex world. For example, many stage-3 individuals expend far too much energy doing things to avoid hurting others' feelings. In doing so, they take personal responsibility for how others experience them. For example, if you know that your parents are disappointed that you abandoned your goal of becoming a physician or an architect, you may internalize their disappointment as *your* problem. Their disappointment becomes a part of how you experience yourself. You may even continue to feel a bit guilty about your career choice, even after you have decided that a career in medicine or architecture is not what's best for you. Your sense of yourself is compromised by how you think your parents view you. This is a psychological burden that can be put aside by individuals at Kegan's stage 4. Stage 4 is about decentering from (making object) a stage-3 embeddedness in shared responsibility and instead applying self-authored principles and personal standards to one's connections, one's shared psychological experiences. For many of us it comes as something of a surprise to learn that it is possible to be a responsible adult and not experience chronic guilt. The stage 3-individual feels guilty precisely because he takes responsibility for others' experiences of him. Only at stage 4 (and in a more primitive way at stage 2) are individuals able to let others take responsibility for their own emotional reactions.

At stage 3, close relationships are exciting and consuming in a way they never were at stage 2. They can also seem suffocating. If you are stage 3, then your experience of yourself is in part a function of how you think your partner, your friends, your co-workers, and your church (or even your waitress) are experiencing you. When how these others experience you is negative, their displeasure becomes a kind of psychological emergency. Consider this example. Imagine for a moment that you come home from work to discover that your partner is angry with you for some real or imagined slight. She says she's too upset to talk about it. How do you react? You may discover that you have a knot in your stomach; you feel awful. And until you can talk all this out and your partner gets over her anger, you will continue to feel bad. Kegan suggests that your continuing bad feelings are a direct result of your making your partner's view or experience of you a part of your experience of yourself (this is what it means to be "subject to" shared psychological experiences). You are caught in the web of your own interpersonalism.

There is an even more fundamental problem with stage-3 interpersonalism. In an important sense you lack a separate and distinct "self" to bring to your relationships. Who you are is someone who works hard to delight your partner, your boss, your friends, your parents, society, your deity, etc. Although this may happen so automatically that you barely notice what you are doing, in every instance you are compelled to be what will be experienced positively by each of these others. You are a "people pleaser." You have pieced out your identity to these multiple mutualities. It can come to feel like a lot of pressure. You begin feeling like everyone owns a piece of you, and you wonder where the "you" is in all of these shared contexts. If you have a relationship with someone who has already transcended shared identities, someone who functions at stage 4, he or she may find trying to get to know you better a slippery affair. That stage-4 person can't really have a relationship with you as a separate individual, because who you are is in part a function of how you believe you are being experienced by that individual. In that important sense you only have a *shared* identity, not a *personal* identity. Your partner may even begin to feel he or she is relating to what is, at least in part, a reflection of his or her own self. Learning to transcend this stage-3 embeddedness in shared perspectives and become truly "oneself" is what the transition to stage 4 is all about. If you are just beginning to start down this path, becoming truly oneself can at first feel like a process of emotional withdrawal. Happily, gaining a distinct and psychologically separate self turns out not to be as isolating as it first feels. As you become more and more distinctly your own person, you eventually get others back as more distinctly themselves, people you can share yourself with, without the burden of believing that what you share has to directly affect the way they feel about themselves. We turn now to a description of Kegan's stage 4.

7 STAGE 4: A SELF-AUTHORED IDENTITY

One of the fundamental longings of human existence is to be true to oneself, to have the sort of psychological independence that allows one to "think for oneself," "be self-sufficient," and feel "whole" and "complete," without the participation of an intimate partner. Kegan's stage 4 is that point in the development of the self. If it takes us twenty or more years to become fully stage 3, it may take another twenty or thirty years to become fully stage 4.[21] And even then, less than half of all highly educated adults seem likely attain a full stage-4 level of functioning.[22] If you are in your early 20s, chances are you are not yet even in transition to Kegan's stage 4. If you are past your middle 20s you may be in a transition to stage 4, but odds are you still function in some situations using a stage-3 way of making meaning. To figure out where you are developmentally (it seems there is something inherently compelling about self knowledge), you will need to understand Kegan's view of the fundamental structure of this later developmental stage.

Looking again at that table in Chapter 3, we can gain a general sense of what Kegan's stage 4 entails. First, whereas the stage-3 individual "co-constructs" himself or herself through shared perspectives (e.g., how I experience myself being experienced by you), the stage-4 individual moves shared experiences over from "subject" to "object." In what is a momentous developmental shift, the stage-4 individual gradually develops the capacity to take a broader, self-authored view of his or her stage-3 shared perspectives. What, then, is the new stage-4 "subject" or perspective? In a nutshell, it's the stage-4 individual's internal system of *personal* values and standards. As happens with all developmental transitions in Kegan's theory, what was previously self-defining (my experience of how I think you experience me) becomes the "object" of a new, broader, more complex way of constructing one's understanding (what *I* think about how I experience you experiencing me). Thus, people who are in part made up by their relationships at stage 3 (*being* one's relationships) move to *having* relationships at Kegan's stage 4. We can get a better understanding of what this means by looking at the contrast between stage-3 and stage-4 intimacy.

As noted above, stage-3 individuals are psychologically embedded in their relationships. When someone they care about is estranged from them, they experience that estrangement directly. They are directly and immediately affected by their emotional conflict with that person. Until they can repair the situation that has alienated them from someone they care about, they experience inner turmoil. They literally may not be able to sleep peacefully until shared feelings of caring are restored. In short, their psychological equilibrium and sense of wholeness is compromised by how important others experience them. There is in this a very palpable psychological dependency (or what some authors in the addictions literature have called "co-dependency"). To be comfortably “yourself,” your partner’s good feelings toward you have to be invoked. And even though at stage 3 you are probably involved in multiple intense, mutually supportive relationships, as I pointed out in the previous chapter, in one important respect you do not actually bring a separate self to those relationships. Whether you bring a composed and confident “self” to a stage-3 relationship depends in part upon how you experience yourself being experienced *in* that relationship. There is another downside to this sort of co-dependency. If you are stage 3, you will tend to hold yourself responsible for how your (presumably stage-3) partners experience themselves in their close encounters with you. You believe (because it is the most sophisticated way you can conceive relationships, when you yourself are still at stage 3) that the affection or disappointment you express to your loved ones becomes incorporated into their experience of themselves. This makes you very careful about what you express to them. If you share with them your disappointment in them, you believe it may make them feel bad about themselves. Yet, if you don’t, and they sense you are holding something back, they may feel that you are not being honest with them. It can end up feeling like a lot of responsibility and pressure. But take heart. Moving to stage 4 fundamentally changes the nature of these sorts of relationship dilemmas.

As I indicated above, the hallmark of stage 4 is psychological independence. Relationships (e.g., “We’re crazy about each other”), societal ideals (e.g., “We should take care of those less fortunate than ourselves"), and personal traits (e.g., "I'm a thoughtful person") are no longer defining (i.e., "subject"). Instead, there is a value-generating self that provides *a perspective on* one's relationships, ideals, and psychological traits. Stage-4 relationships are different (e.g., "I love the way you look at the world."), as are societal ideals (e.g., "It's important to me to provide myself with opportunities to help people less fortunate than I am"), and personal traits (e.g., "I like to be able to think of myself as a thoughtful person"). Because stage-4 individuals are no longer subject to or psychologically co-defined by their relationships, shared ideals, or internal traits, it is probably the case that they may appear to experience intimate relationships with less emotional immediacy than do stage-3 individuals. After all, if how you experience me no longer *directly* and immediately affects my sense of self (because I've progressed to stage 4), then in one sense I psychologically have less at stake in my relationship with you. But if *you* are still at stage 3, you may experience my growing psychological independence as a sign that I no longer care about you with the intensity that I did in the past. Arguably, I do, in fact, care about you just as strongly, but the "you" I care about has been transformed by my new developmental capacity. From viewing you as in part made up by my love for you, I have moved to a position where I can see you as a person who has your own identity, an identity that is (or eventually will be) independent of my experience of you. My sense of you and of myself is liberated from our experience of each other. I now see you for more of who you are (or have the potential to be in the future, if you are still not at stage 4). In short, I see you as a psychologically separate person, or at least as someone who is becoming a psychologically separate person. This greater psychological independence does not mean that I am any less committed to you and to my other close relationships. Indeed, many stage-4 individuals place the maintenance and nurturance of their intimate relationships at the very center of their personal value system.

You may recall that stage-2 individuals also view others as separate and distinct from themselves. As a result, we may at times view the stage-2 person's ability to function independently, to "not care what others think about them," as a virtue. But stage-2 independence in relationships is a far cry from stage-4 independence. At stage 2, I understand that you have your own *separate* needs and desires, so I can see you as a kind of independent operator, someone who "does her own thing." But at stage 2, I do not yet have the capacity to see you, for example, as someone who routinely transcends your narrow self-interest for the sake of your connections to others or in the service of your cherished ideals. I do not, therefore, grant to you some of your most important attributes. This is, of course, one of the reasons that relationships with stage-2 individuals are less than fully satisfying (unless you are stage 2 yourself). Let me give an example. Some years ago, I had administrative responsibility for my academic department, and one of my faculty members came to me with a proposal to fund his travel to an unsuitable out-of-town meeting. When I raised questions about the legitimacy of his request, he assured me that I could also use university funds for similar travel for myself. I remember thinking, "Who does he think I am? I'm not the sort of person who would put my personal desires ahead of the legitimate policies of the university." In retrospect, I now see that this man was operating at his stage-2 limit, and so he imagined that I must be stage 2 also. In fact, I was probably a solid stage 3 at the time. I felt offended. But in reality, he was merely projecting his own stage-2 orientation onto me. It was a perfectly natural thing for him to do. My point is, stage-2 "independence" in an adult may look appealing at first. But when you look into it, it's pretty simplistic. Stage-4 independence, in contrast, has a great deal more to recommend it because it is value driven, not self-interested.

Despite its greater sophistication, it can be argued that the stage-4 way of experiencing close relationships is less "romantic" than is the stage-3 experience. But in practice, close relationships are no less engaging at stage 4 than they are at stage 3. In one sense, stage-4 relationships may be even closer, even more intimate, than are stage-3 relationships. Rainer M. Rilke, quoted in Kegan,[23] describes stage-4 intimacy as follows:

> Once the realization is accepted that even between the closest human beings infinite distances continue to exist, a wonderful living side by side can grow up, if they succeed in loving the distance between them which makes it possible for each to see the

> other whole against the sky.

If you have achieved the psychological independence of stage 4, you are no longer forced (by the way you structure reality) to experience me as a kind of psychological mirror for yourself. Instead, you can step back and see me "whole against the sky." Kegan provides his own description of stage-4 intimacy, based on being able to psychologically "visit" another person who has his or her own, personal way of constructing meaning.[24]

> Like respectful and enlightened anthropologists, they regularly visit, and deeply appreciate, the other's "culture of mind" (independent and unique view of reality). At their best, they suspend the tendency to evaluate the other's "culture" through the lens of their own, and seek rather to discover the terms by which the other is shaping meaning or creating value. Not only does each seem to benefit from frequent "travel" to the other's "culture," but the one who is "being visited" also seems to appreciate the experience of having the other come in with a non-imperial stance to see how reality is being constructed.

I think these two quotations illustrate once again how *structural* development, of the sort described by Robert Kegan, is a process in which stepping back from the perspective in which one was previously embedded permits one to see more of the complexity that was there all along. This is true whether one is talking about a six-year-old making his perceptions of liquid in a beaker "object" of a new understanding of the conservation of matter or a forty-year-old beginning to let his spouse's feelings toward him be *her* feelings, not a part of *his* feelings toward himself. To repeat that wonderful quote from the frontispiece, "What the eye sees better, the heart feels more deeply."[25]

In illustrating distinctions between stage-3 and stage-4 construction of experience, I have emphasized how such differences might affect *interpersonal* relationships. But one's developmental level affects more than the narrowly interpersonal. There are equally profound differences in self-reflectiveness and idealism between stages 3 and 4. Recall that individuals who reach stage 3 are able to reflect upon their own psychological (as opposed to their behavioral) qualities. Stated another way, individuals at stage 3 can create an *abstract* sense of their identity. So, for example, they may say they are "sensitive" or "confident" or "caring" (all stage-3 abstractions) as opposed to the more concrete stage-2 identities of "liking to ski," or "wanting to help others." What, then, is the nature of the self-awareness of individuals who have achieved stage 4? Kegan suggests that at stage 4 people gain an internal sense of self-regulation, self-formation, and autonomy. In contrast to many stage-3 individuals, there is a sense of coherence or consistency across different psychological contexts. The stage-4 individual, for example, no longer feels like an "obedient child" (or rebellious child), when visiting parents, and then a "trusted and valued friend" when back home. The stage-4 sense of self has cohered and stabilized, because it is created by a self system that no longer requires another's point of view to achieve wholeness (as was true back at stage 3). The stage-4 individual has a more stable and consistent sense of self, regardless of the context (visiting parents versus being at home with friends). I'll try to illustrate this by describing one of the ways I have changed as a teacher over the past 30 years.

Some years ago my sense of adequacy as a classroom instructor was a direct function of how I thought students were experiencing my teaching. Students looking bored or confused directly elicited in me feelings of inadequacy. Years later (remember, Kegan suggests that it may take as many as 20 years or more to fully move to stage 4 from stage 3), my experience of myself in the classroom is quite different. Whether students look bored or confused (or are falling asleep) is still highly relevant "data" or information. But it no longer has a *direct* impact on my experience of myself. Now, functioning at stage 4, my students' looks of boredom or confusion get processed by me through my own personal set of standards about what I think constitutes good teaching. I may decide, upon reflecting about the origin of my students' boredom, that I am not meeting *my own* standards of good teaching. In that case, I may end up feeling just as "bad" about my teaching as I did when I was a stage-3 instructor. Alternatively, I may conclude that last weekend's Alabama game and associated festivities has taken its toll on a number of my students. And they, not me, are responsible for their inattentiveness. There's a key difference here. When I was stage 3, my students' reactions had a *direct* and immediate impact on my sense of self. I was co-constructing my identity with my perception of my students' experiences of me. Now, years later as a stage-4 instructor, the impact is *indirect*. Stated in "structural" terms, how I experienced students' experience of me was "subject" at stage 3. Their experience of me gradually got moved over to "object" as I progressed (finally!) to stage 4. Now I'm the one deciding whether to feel good about my teaching. The contrast in what it feels like to be in front of a room full of students is profound.

Readers struggling to understand Kegan's theory for the first time often have difficulty understanding the distinction between stage-3 "idealism" and stage-4 "ideology." Both stage-3 and stage-4 individuals have no difficulty in articulating their "personal beliefs." But the underlying structure of those beliefs is quite different. At stage 3, one's beliefs are "co-constructed." That is, they entail identification with ideas and principles that exist "out there" in one's particular social or societal context. One is connected to certain ideas and principles, but, at stage 3, those ideas and principles are not wholly one's own. To know if one is living up to one's stage-3 ideals, the stage-3 person checks her actions against a consensual or socially shared standard. Not so at stage 4. At stage 4 one has taken a variety of stage-3 ideals and fashioned them into a personal ideology. How can you tell the difference? Stage-4 individuals will explain in *personal* terms why they believe what they believe (e.g., "In my experience, it's always better to first consider the possibility that the other person may be correct."). The stage-3 individual will ultimately justify their beliefs in *shared* terms, in relationship to an external standard (e.g, "The Bible teaches us that one should turn the other cheek."). It's this personal system of sense making that permits me, as a stage-4 instructor, to come to my *own* conclusion when I look out and see bored or distracted faces in my classroom. If you're feeling a bit confused, don't get discouraged. It gets a little tricky, because both stage-3 and stage-4 individuals have "values." Think of it this way: Only stage-4 individuals have what Kegan calls "values about values."[26] I'm an Episcopalian. And the Episcopal Church takes positions on a variety of social, ethical, and religious issues. I'm OK with most of those positions. See what I just did? I implied that there is a place I "stand" where I have my own take on what the Church teaches. If you're stage 4, and religious, it helps if your church thinks it's important for you to "think for yourself" about these sorts of issues.

Stage 4 Has Limitations Too. There are a number of attractions of stage 4. One big attraction is that stage 4 represents the achievement of psychological autonomy. As shown in the table back in chapter 3, the lens through which the stage-4 individual constructs meaning is a personally authored system of values and principles. Psychological independence and psychological "adulthood" have been achieved. (And if you are thinking, "That suggests that some people never do become *psychological* adults," you are correct.) For many adults, struggling to free themselves from the "co-dependency" of stage 3, stage-4's autonomy may seem like a psychological promised land. But as is true with earlier stages, stage 4 has its own inherent limitations. Kegan describes those limitations thus:

> If the strength of the institutional balance is its autonomy, it would be as true to say that its weakness lies in its embeddedness in this autonomy. Its self-naming and self-nourishing converts the world within its reach to operatives on behalf of its personal enterprise. What is experienced from within the balance (i.e., within stage 4) as independence and self-regulation might as accurately be seen from beyond the balance as a kind of psychological isolation . . . .[27]

In short, others may find the stage-4 individual to be overly self-contained. And indeed, even the stage-4 individual may begin to experience him or herself that way. The problem lies with the stage-4 individual's embeddedness in or inability to take a perspective on his or her personally constructed self-system. If you are going to be in a relationship with a stage-4 individual, then you are going to have to see her as an autonomous value generator. And to be true to herself, the stage-4 person will relate to you through that self-system. Kegan suggests that, as a result, others often feel like the relationship is being "mediated" through the other's constructed, stage-4 identity. It's as if you can't get through the stage-4 person's psychological "edifice" to connect with them directly and emotionally. Instead, the stage-4 person seems almost to be walled off behind an elaborate, self-constructed identity. The self-system or self-authored psychological edifice of stage 4 is what prompted Kegan in his 1982 book to call stage 4 the "Institutional Self". You can think of the stage-4 person as a kind of CEO of their self-system. They're in charge; they make the decisions; and they hold themselves responsible for the consequences.

To help you sort out the achievements and limitations of the three most common adult stages (stages 2, 3, & 4) these are summarized below.

Stage	Achievements	Limitations
2 "Imperial"	Control over one's impulses; a stable sense of self; can take another's point of view; able to meet fixed (concrete) role expectations	Centered in own needs and interests; unable to enter into the shared mutuality of interpersonalism or idealism; no subjective self to share with others
3 "Interpersonal"	Relativizes own self interest to the care of a relationship or to the collective good; able to be idealistic; has an internal life to share with others	The self is parceled out to various mutualities; no inner compass; lacks self determination and cannot grant it to others
4 "Institutional"	Self authoring; able to be thoughtful and objective about others' theories, identities	Defensive about perceived inconsistencies between one's actions and core values; relationships are not direct -- they are mediated through the self system

The Achievements and Limitations of Kegan's Most Common Adult Stages (Adapted from Kegan, 1982; 1994)

I'm guessing that a question that has occurred to you is what intimate relationships are like when two people are at different stages. In particular, what about relationships where one person is stage 4 and the other stage 3? Aren't those relationships problematic? After all, if only the stage-4 partner can see the other "whole against the sky," isn't there a fatal asymmetry in stage-3/stage-4 relationships? I think the answer depends, in part, on whether one views these relationships in static or in developmental terms. Let's assume for a moment that you're the stage-4 party in such a relationship. You can't help noticing that you and your partner bring a different awareness and sensitivity to your relationship. Your stage-3 partner is much more sensitive to how he or she thinks he or she is being experienced by others, and, depending on how expressive you are, to how you feel about him or her. Your stage-3 partner may require considerably more expressions of your caring than you do theirs.

And it's also likely that both of you have noticed this asymmetry. It may worry your partner that you seem more self-assured and less affected by these expressions than he is. And as a result you find yourself feeling slightly parental with someone to whom you really just want to feel close. It may also concern you that your partner's emotional equilibrium is sometimes so vulnerable to real or imagined betrayals or slights. It really would be nice if your partner could just get over all this concern with how everyone, including you, is experiencing him. What's more, confusing you with his experience of you, your partner doesn't seem to be able to see you "whole against the sky," and at some level that leaves you feeling cut off from the deepest part of who you consider yourself to be. What are you to make of all this? Here's where I think the views presented in this book can help.

Lacking a developmental perspective, it's easy to begin to think that the two of you have grown apart. Or worse, you may begin thinking that what you have discovered is a previously hidden but fundamental incompatibility. Such a view of your partner is too static. Instead of realizing that your partner is caught in a particular moment in what Kegan calls "life's motion," you mistake who your partner is at this moment in time for who he or she will always be. In fact, like all of us, your partner is in motion, and if you can see that larger person in motion, there is a sympathy that can grow up for their struggles and a delight that can emerge in sharing in his or her forward progress. Hanging in there with someone who has the potential of catching up to you is a lot different from trying to decide if you really want to settle for someone who is not who you thought he or she was when you fell in love. It's still a tough call, but at least the call honors more of who you both are and who you both, hopefully, will become.

Now I'm guessing that you have a couple of other questions. What, you may be thinking, do I do if *I'm* the person who's stage 3, and my partner's probably stage 4? Or, if I pegged you correctly with my initial example, you're wondering if there's anything you can do to help your stage-3 partner move along more quickly or even something you can do to help them get started moving. Because you may not be seeing much forward motion there. You may not like my answer, but the biggest thing you can do is to start seeing them in developmental terms. So let me finish up my description of the stages with a brief description of stage 5. Then in chapter 9 I'll take up, at least in general terms, the question of what Kegan sees as facilitating developmental change.

8 STAGE 5: BEYOND PSYCHOLOGICAL AUTONOMY

Before attempting a summary of Kegan's final stage, it should be acknowledged that trying to describe stage 5 is a bit of a stretch for me. First, most adults have not yet reached Kegan's stage 4. At best, the decades from 25 to 55 are characterized by the slow process of moving shared perspectives over from subject to object and developing a new "subject" or "organizing process" based on self-authored values and principles. Grappling with the limitations of full stage-4 functioning is years off. And stage-4 functioning is highly supported in our culture,[28] so there is often little external pressure to move past stage 4. In fact, researchers have found few individuals who are in the transition to stage 5, and no study I know about has actually identified anyone who is functioning at stage 5[29]. One implication of the low incidence of stage-5 functioning is that many of us are not likely to have a clear understanding of the nature of stage-5 perspective-taking. Most of us will, of course, construct some sort of understanding of what stage 5 is all about, but it is apt to be a stage-2 or stage-3 or stage-4 understanding of stage 5. In short, there may be more to stage 5 than we are able to grasp from our current developmental positions. Recognizing these inherent difficulties, the following description of stage 5 will be shorter than my treatment of the other stages.

Following the fundamental logic of constructive-developmental change, Kegan's stage 5 will result in the organizing process ("subject") of stage 4 being moved over to "object" at stage 5. What does this mean? In an important way, it means that the competent operation of one's self-system (the "subject" of stage 4) becomes something that one *does* rather than an expression of something that one *is*. Our autonomous running of ourselves becomes "relativized"; it is no longer paramount to our meaning-making. Instead, there is *a self that creates selves*. The emerging stage-5 self is suspicious of the stage-4 notion that any particular "ideological" self is actually all that one might be. What, then, is the new stage-5 "subject" or self that has begun to decenter from the old, stage-4 self? Answering this question is where things begin to get a bit fuzzy.

Recall that Kegan suggests that at stage 4 people have an autonomous self that they bring to their relationships. The stage-4 self creates and enters into relationships. At stage 5 the process is reversed. Relationships give rise to the self. Stated somewhat differently, it is the process of creating or "inventing" ourselves, as experienced in intense relationships, that begins to become subject, the source of the stage-5 self. One is no longer a particular institutional self. One is the creator of that self. The new "subject" or self is the *creative process*, not what is being created. A sign that one may be moving from stage 4 to stage 5 is how one experiences data that suggest that one's self-authored identity is not working well. At stage 4 such information is irritating and necessitates actions to further shore up and restore the integrity of the threatened self-system. At stage 5 such information is not only tolerated, it is embraced as an opportunity to discover more of what one *is* in the process of becoming. The emerging stage-5 self recognizes itself in the *process* of becoming, where incompleteness is taken to be a fact of psychological existence. The old stage-4 self-system or self-authored identity becomes "object" where it can be put on, like a familiar old sweater, as circumstances demand. But that sweater (the stage-4 identity) is not the self, it is something the self can "wear" as needed. Kegan describes the distinction between stage 4 and stage 5 as follows:

> Where the institutional balance has a wariness about losing the stability and self-subsistence of "the form" (personal or public), the interindividual balance (stage 5) is more likely to be wary about losing sight of the temporary, preliminary, and self-constructed quality of any particular form.[30]

Indeed, Kegan suggests that stage-5 individuals may ". . . seek out contradictions by which to nourish the ongoing process of (their) reconstruction."[31] Contradiction and paradox are not puzzles to be solved, they are understood to be part and parcel of human existence. A summary of Kegan's view of stage-5 functioning is presented in the following table.

The Interindividual Self (Stage 5)	
The Interpersonal Self (Nature of Relations) Able to be deeply intimate and explore aspects of identity created through relationships. Intimacy that is not mediated through a particular self-system; intimacy which is immediate.	The Intrapersonal Self (Sense of Self/Reality) Trans-ideological/Post-ideological. Sees experience as fundamentally dynamic and evolving. The self and stage-4 ideologies are elements in a kaleidoscope of constantly changing patterns.

Characteristics of Stage 5 (From Kegan, 1994)

Achievement of stage-5 meaning-making undoubtedly alters the way one views others. At stage 4 we enjoy a sort of *mano-a-mano* interchange with those others whom we perceive to also be at stage 4. It's a kind of "I'm me, and you're you" experience. It feels good interacting with someone who knows who he or she is and who recognizes me as someone who knows who I am. We don't have to tiptoe around one another, constrained by that old stage-3 concern that each could be directly affected by how the other sees him. We're all about expressing and defending our cherished ideas and ideals. But I imagine this all begins to change when one starts the progression to stage 5. If I perceive that you are no longer identified with a particular self-system, then I can no longer encounter you as that system. I have to begin to look past whatever identity you are "wearing" – devoted spouse, ethical humanist, thoughtful professional, irresponsible hedonist, etc. – to a self that is a creator of those identities. It's in that self-creating process that I may encounter more of who you are now becoming. Surface identities serve only to separate us. This line of thinking is what prompted Kegan to assert that “true intimacy” occurs only at stage 5.[32] Still sound pretty fuzzy? If so, I suspect you’ll do better if you look for descriptions of what may be stage 5 in the writings of some of the religious mystics. This sounds to me like a task for our later years.

9 THE DYNAMICS OF DEVELOPMENTAL CHANGE

Arriving at an understanding of Kegan's stages of the development of the self is a challenging undertaking. We are not accustomed to focusing on ways in which we and others structure or "construct" experience. We tend to focus instead on the experience that has been constructed. And as we begin to understand what Kegan's stages are all about, we often experience a sense of relief that we have begun to master this complex new view of human experience. A sure sign that the theory is beginning to register is that we find ourselves wondering about the developmental stage of friends and loved ones and in particular our own stage level. It may not be welcome news, therefore, to learn that a major component of Kegan's theory has been neglected in most of the preceding summary. Kegan's theory is not so much about stages as it is about the ongoing process of gaining and then losing successive ways of making sense of experience. Reflecting this emphasis on developmental "motion" and the *dynamic* equilibrium at each of the stages, Kegan at times calls them "balances" or "truces,"[33] not stages. And even though there are no definitive data on how long we spend at each stage relative to how long we spend in transitions from one stage to the next, a significant portion of our lives is probably spent in the transitions. And as much as Kegan's description of the "deep structure" of the stages illuminates personal and interpersonal phenomena, the psychological dynamics of transition shines its own light on the experience of being human.

Different psychology theorists have different ideas about what stimulates people to move from one stage to the next. For Sigmund Freud the impetus was internal, the predictable maturation of the body's expression of and physical location of the sexual instincts. Erik Erikson, in contrast, gave greater emphasis to the successive challenges presented by the society within which our psychosexuality is being expressed. Such differing views of the *causes* of developmental change are relevant and important because they provide insights into how human beings move from infantile immaturity to adult maturity. They can also help us understand why different individuals acquire maturity at different rates and to different levels, and how developmental changes can be facilitated, if at all. Both Freud and Erikson believed that progression from one developmental stage to the next was inevitable and (provided one doesn't die prematurely) universal. Freud's view was that we are pushed on through successive developmental stages by internally arising biological maturation. For Erikson, it is largely (though not entirely) society that pushes us through the stages. In both theories, "fixation" doesn't mean that development has stopped, only that the issues of a particular stage were not adequately resolved. This means that an individual can have fixations at more than one stage at the same time.

Jean Piaget's stages of cognitive development and Kegan's

stages of the development of the self follow a different logic. In these "constructive/developmental" theories, one does not progress to the next stage unless the present stage has been fully achieved. So, for example, adults who fail to master Kegan's stage 2 will *not* progress to his stage 3. This is the case because the deep structure of each stage in these theories is a more complicated reconstruction of the elements of the preceding stage. If the elements are not fully there, they can't be reconstructed. One has to have learned how to construct reality using the "deep structure" of one's current stage before development to the next stage is possible. But failure to acquire the structures of one's current stage is not the only reason a person may not progress to the next meaning-making stage. Some individuals may not progress because their *environment* is not challenging enough to make the development of a more complex view of experience necessary. If, for example, you have a teenager who spends most of his leisure time playing computer games by himself, and you, as his parent, have a clear set of rules and consequences about how he is to conduct himself at home, there's little need for him to develop a meaning-making framework beyond the stage-2 capacity to play roles, follow rules, and keep one's impulses under control. This hypothetical teenager may be fully stage 2, but he is unlikely to progress toward stage 3 unless his environment gets more complicated.

"Complicated" here means that to cope effectively your teenager will need to be able to construct a more complex view of his world. It follows that one of the factors that is essential for developmental change in Kegan's subject/object theory is challenge, or what Kegan terms "disconfirmation." Disconfirmation is the experience of social and interpersonal demands that require a more complicated view of experience than the individual currently possesses. Not all new environmental demands are more complicated. So, for example, you may decide to change the contingencies on your teenager's behavior or increase the scope of his household chores. But none of this is more "complicated," because it can still be perfectly understood from a stage-2 perspective, a perspective that sees the world as a place where one has to do what *others* want you to do so that they will provide you with what *you* want. Disconfirmation, in contrast, entails a *qualitative* (not quantitative) change in demands. An example from my own experience in parenting may help clarify what this means.

When my daughter was fifteen, I experienced growing frustration with her lack of consideration for other family members. Efforts to revise her chores to include more tasks that contributed to the smooth functioning of the family did little to alter my sense that she acted more like a tenant who was performing certain chores to pay for her room and board than a member of the family. Having recently read Kegan's first book, I decided to implement a change in how her allowance was structured. I gave her a large enough increase in her allowance to get her attention and then told her that the old system of money in exchange for household chores was being abolished. As a "member of the family" and in recognition of her greater maturity and independence, she was entitled to a portion of the family's monetary resources. But at the same time, I reminded her that she needed to try to show other members of the family more consideration and take others' feelings and needs into account in deciding how to be a better family member. Without going into the details, this new approach resulted in significant changes in my daughter's participation in family life. The desired behavior change occurred. But more importantly, her sense of herself in relation to the family also changed. I have to admit, however, that this sort of rapid change is unusual. It is likely that my daughter was already moving into stage 3 in her relationships with her peers, so she was able to use her emerging stage-3 capacity for mutuality with her friends to "reconstruct" her relationship to her family. Indeed, one could argue that her family environment had remained too simply structured for too long and had not provided enough "disconfirmation" of her stage-2 meaning-making.

The Concept of the "Holding Environment." In describing the dynamics of developmental change, Kegan draws upon psychoanalyst Donald Winnicott's concept of the "holding environment." I like that term and the image it evokes of a parent lovingly holding his infant. But the term also refers, for example, to how many parents lovingly "hold" their growing adolescents and how one's profession can nurture the development of self-authorship. Kegan describes the holding environment as an interpersonal and cultural context that is *attuned to* the person's current developmental capability and provides neither too much nor too little support for that current level of capability. The elements of an adequate holding environment necessarily change as the person being "held" grows in capability. For example, as parents we know it is our job to protect our toddlers from their impulsivity. But as our toddlers develop their *own* capacity to control their impulses, we must sensitively relinquish *our* control of their impulsivity to them. In this sense, a good holding environment is characterized by its recognition of the changing structural capabilities of the person being held.

There is a second key feature of holding environments. A good holding environment recognizes where the person being "held" is headed developmentally and is capable of shifting the nature of its "holding" to anticipate those emerging developmental changes. We must have a feel for what comes next in the person's developmental journey. This is what prompted Kegan to observe that merely loving one's children is not sufficient for ensuring their healthy development. One also has to alter the expression of that love as our children mature. We must not only see our children for who they are at present; it is also important to see them for who they are about to become. In other words, an effective holding environment not only recognizes and supports the person's *current* highest capability, it also invites some movement *beyond* that capability. One of Kegan's notable contributions to the understanding of the development of the self is his articulation of a *series* of holding environments or, as he terms them, "cultures of embeddedness" across the developmental lifespan.[34] Each of us, no matter our age and developmental stage, needs such an environment within which we can be ourselves and, when it is time, begin to reconstruct ourselves into an even "larger" self.

Above I noted that adequate holding environments are not static. Rather than merely "holding" a person where they are developmentally, a good holding environment recognizes and promotes movement toward the person's next step in the evolution of their meaning making. In Kegan's terminology, an effective holding environment offers both "confirmation" and "disconfirmation." In colloquial terms, the holding environment gives us the message "I know where you're coming from" (confirmation) but then adds "and I know you can do a little better" (disconfirmation). The following table summarizes the confirmations and disconfirmations of the effective holding environments for each of Kegan's developmental stages. One way of thinking about what constitutes an adequate holding environment is to see it as providing just a little bit less external structure than the person is able to generate for himself or herself at his or her present level of development. This creative gap then becomes the gap into which the person grows. It is, of course, possible to make the gap too large. For example, most sexually active early teenagers, who are expected to use condoms to avoid contracting AIDS, lack the structural capacity to regulate their current sexual desires by using their knowledge of dire future consequences. A "culture" that expects them to do so is not an effective holding environment, because the gap between capability (stage 2) and external requirements (making a possible future a part of one's *present* reality) is too great.

STAGE	CONFIRMATION	DISCONFIRMATION
Incorporative (0)	Physical holding, eye contact, attunement to infant's immediate needs	Doesn't meet child's every need, stops nursing, recognizes emerging willfulness
Impulsive (1)	Support's child's use of fantasy and intense, self-centered attachments, rivalries, and impulses	Holds child responsible for her feelings, fantasies, and impulses; asserts own independence from child's needs
Imperial (2)	Supports displays of self-sufficiency, competence and rule following	Denies validity of seeing others only as holders of separate interests; demands mutuality, respect
Interpersonal (3)	Acknowledges capacity for self-sacrifice, mutuality, self-reflection, and internal subjectivity	Refuses to be fused with other's self while still remaining in relationship; invites other's psychological independence
Institutional (4)	Supports capacity for independence and self-sufficiency	Refuses to accept relationships mediated through a fixed identity
Interindividual(5)	Supports self-surrender	

Confirming and Contradicting Functions of Holding Environments For Each of Kegan's 6 Developmental Stages (adapted from Kegan, 1982, Pp. 118-120)

10 A Good Holding Environment Also Entails Sticking Around

Kegan adds a third component to his view of holding environments. This component, what Kegan terms "continuity," is of a different order than confirmation and contradiction. Confirmation and contradiction are responses provided by the members of one's holding environment in the present moment. Continuity, in contrast, has an inherently enduring aspect. "Continuity" is defined by Kegan as the holding environment "staying put," so that it can be reintegrated by the person after he or she has moved to a new level of meaning making. In describing continuity Kegan quotes the early twentieth century humorist Mark Twain: "My parents were so dumb when I was seventeen and so much smarter when I was twenty-one; I can't believe how much they learned in just four years."[35] The humor here is, of course, that its the adolescent who has changed, not the parents. But notice that the parents have "stayed put" in a psychological sense, so that they could be reconstructed with what was probably their adolescent's newly discovered stage-3 capacity. Kegan's theory suggests that with the achievement of each new stage's more complex frame for viewing the world, we see complexities that were there all along but which were hidden from our view. The risk of a lack of continuity for Mark Twain's late adolescent was that he could have "left" his parents while he was using his old meaning-making and never "rediscovered" them while using his new way of making-meaning.

Fortunately, Twain's parents stuck around so they could be "rediscovered." In most instances, parents are pretty good at providing this critical holding-environment quality of "continuity." This is not always the case with other, non-parental, holding environments.

As an example of the failure of this third function, Kegan decries what he terms "serial relationships," a common feature of modern culture, a feature that undermines the "continuity" function of holding environments.[36] Too often, as one party to a close relationship gains the new perspective of a higher stage (typically, stage 3 or stage 4), he or she feels increasingly estranged from the old partner (the partner, in turn, may feel abandoned). The evolving partner is beginning to make meaning in a way that the other partner is not capable of fully understanding. So the evolving partner moves on to a new relationship in which the new partner is better able to "re-cognize" him or her at the new stage than could the partner who has been left behind. This pattern is problematical in at least two important ways. Lacking a true developmental perspective on intimate relationships, we often fail to see the likelihood that our partners may eventually catch up with us. Instead, partly because our newly developing way of constructing reality is fragile in its newness, we experience our partner's appeals to the old way of constructing the relationship (and us in that relationship) as a threat to our emerging new identity. What we often fail to understand is that even though we have begun to "outgrow" our partner, chances are our partner will eventually "catch up." The second problem with "serial relationships" is that they often reflect a static view of intimacy. When our feelings for one another change, we are apt to experience this change as a sign that we are no longer "in love," as if the nature of being in love never changes. Utilizing the developmental perspective summarized in this book, Kegan suggests the following as a better understanding of longterm intimate relationships.

> Just as a person is not a stage of development but the process of development itself, a marriage contract is not, ideally, a particular evolutionary contract but a context for continued evolution. If it is not, the marriage may give out at the same time the evolutionary truce gives out. . . . If one partner enters and constructs a marriage from the interpersonal balance (stage 3), for example, and then begins to emerge from this embeddedness, the marriage itself becomes, or needs to become, something new. (The marriage) that may have been a context for exercising and celebrating . . . (stage 3) affiliation, nurturance, and identification might have to become something more like a context for loving which preserves, supports, and celebrates a kind of (stage 4) mutual distinctness, independence, or cooperation of separate interests.[37]

To summarize, a holding environment has three qualities: confirmation, disconfirmation, and continuity. When things are going well, the people and social institutions of our holding environment recognize us in our current stage of evolution, let us know that the world (and we ourselves) are more complex than we now perceive them to be, and stick around so we can assimilate our old understanding of the important people in our lives to our new way of making sense of the world. There is a lot to be said for creating and living in communities that share these features.

11 DEVELOPMENTAL CHANGE IS INHERENTLY STRESSFUL

Kegan suggests that developmental change is inherently stressful. From a constructive/developmental perspective, moving from one's current developmental stage to the next initially feels like the loss of one's stable and familiar sense of self. The old self is, at first, repudiated while the new self ("subject") has not yet been consolidated. Or as Kegan suggests, one must lose one's mind on the way to gaining a new mind. In the midst of these sorts of developmental transitions there can be substantial distress and risk. Kegan illustrates his view of the risks inherent in developmental transitions by clarifying the causes of "pathological" depression. Depression is a common and normal reaction to loss. What is *not* normal (i.e., is pathological) is depression that fails to subside after passage of a reasonable amount of time. Put another way, why is it that some individuals appear to be able to work their way through significant losses while others appear to become stuck in their grief? The answer often lies, according to Kegan, in the timing of the loss. Losses that occur early in a developmental transition are more likely to produce prolonged depression and anxiety than are losses that occur either later in the transition or during periods of psychological "balance." In both instances one can operate comfortably (at least at times) using a particular stage of meaning-making. But early in developmental transitions one has given up an old meaning-making structure, while not yet having mastered a new one. When one experiences a loss at these times, there may be no satisfactory way to make the world cohere.

An example may help the reader understand this idea. Some years ago one of the author's cousins, a successful salesman in his mid forties, seemed firmly entrenched in a stage-2 way of viewing his relationships and himself. He was economically successful, and he defined himself in terms of all the things he could do and acquire: fancy cars, boats, a house in the suburbs, and an attractive new wife. Life was good. His marital relationship was all about doing with his wife those things that both enjoyed doing (a stage-2 construction of marital happiness). But a year or two into the marriage a change began to take place. He began to talk differently about his relationship with his wife. Knowing that I was a psychologist, he tried to describe what was becoming different about his marriage. He began describing his wife as his "special friend" and noting how they were amazingly similar, not in terms of what they wanted or liked doing (a stage-2 embeddedness), but in terms of what they *felt* about each other and what they were *thinking*. This emerging focus on shared internal experience seemed to be the leading edge of stage-3 mutuality. It was new, exciting, and powerfully engaging for this middle-aged man. Then, out of the blue, his wife left him for another man. He was devastated and sank into a deep depression that took him nearly two years to overcome. Why was the loss of his wife so powerful? Why wasn't he able to write her off as unworthy of him and move on? Kegan suggests that the answer lies in the vulnerability inherent in developmental transitions. This man, entranced by a powerful new experience of mutuality, had begun to leave his old stage-2 imperialism behind. What he could acquire and what he could accomplish in the world of business no longer seemed paramount. Material success had lost its centrality. In structural terms, he was no longer "subject to" his needs, interests, and agendas. Instead, he was beginning to construct and experience a "new" reality, a reality that was co-constructed with his wife's reality (i.e., stage 3). But his emerging capacity to construct meaning in terms of stage 3 mutuality was being exercised *exclusively* within his marital relationship. When that relationship suddenly ended, he literally found himself without the other half of his emerging sense of self. With no other stage-3 relationships within which to recreate his emerging self, he found himself in a desolate psychological no-man's-land. His loss was not so much the loss of a loved one as it was a loss of the one context that was letting him become an exiting new self. In a psychological sense, when he lost his partner, he lost himself. The severity and duration of his resulting depression was not merely a function of how much he loved his wife. It was more fundamentally due to loss of the one context in which he could make his new (stage-3) identity cohere. He had lost himself!

I want to make one final observation about my cousin that may at first appear to be directed only to therapists and counselors.

But this observation is intended for laypersons and counselors alike, and it has to do with the importance of having a lifespan developmental perspective when trying to sort out the dynamics of emotional issues. Too many counselors and psychotherapists, in my view, would tend to view my cousin as having failed to develop a separate sense of self during early childhood. And some mental health professionals might even have diagnosed my depressed cousin as having "borderline personality" features. (If you are unfamiliar with this term, suffice it to say that it is not a kind thing to say about someone, as it suggests the person is suffering from deep-seated personality flaws rooted in early childhood.) Kegan critiques the common view that a person's problems in maintaining a separate identity are necessarily rooted in difficulties in his or her earliest childhood relationships.[38] Instead, Kegan argues that development entails *recurring* themes of separation-individuation that appear throughout the lifespan. Later "separation-individuation" problems, of the sort experienced by my cousin, are not necessarily a repetition of, or reemergence of, childhood difficulties. Each new separation-individuation issue may, in fact, be qualitatively different from the issue as it was encountered at earlier stages. This is an important distinction, particularly for counselors and therapists. There is an enormous difference in how one should treat an adult who never separated psychologically from his mother in earliest childhood (the "borderline personality") and an adult who has encountered difficulties while moving from preadolescent imperialism (stage 2) to adolescent/early-adult interpersonalism (stage 3). In the former instance, one is dealing with deep-seated developmental delay; in the latter instance with disruptions of adolescent or early adulthood developmental progression. It is important to be able to distinguish the two. I would not have wanted my cousin to seek therapy from someone who viewed his problems as having their origin in early childhood. My cousin didn't need to figure out how to be more psychologically independent from his mother, he needed help in learning how to be more connected to others in a stage-3 manner. His depression was the leading edge of an exciting developmental change, not a symptom of deep-seated childhood difficulties.

Before moving on to other issues related to developmental change, I want to address one other implication of the idea that developmental progression is inherently stressful. Most of us, including most mental health professionals, view psychological distress as something to be relieved or removed. When someone we care about (or are counseling as part of a professional relationship) is feeling anxious or depressed, our natural impulse is to try to do something to help the individual overcome the distress and return to his or her former sense of well-being. But viewed from a constructive-developmental perspective, this may be exactly the wrong thing to do. If we focus only on relieving the individual's distress, on restoring someone's previous equilibrium, we are, in effect, aligning ourselves with a familiar but increasingly outworn self, a self that, at least initially, views the distress as a kind of "not-me" experience. In doing so, we are failing to "hold" a larger person who is in the process of becoming someone who will soon be able to make sense of himself or herself and his or her life experiences in a new and more articulated manner. What we should be doing, instead of helping them get rid of their anxiety, is helping them own their distress as a natural part of a significant developmental transition. As Kegan puts it, responding by attempting to relieve a person's anxiety ". . . reconfirms the me-I-have-been at the expense of the me-I-am-becoming."[39] When we are able to tolerate another's distress and be "good company" during a developmental transition, we are giving someone a far greater gift than temporary relief from their distress. Reflecting upon this point, I have to admit to wondering to what extent our culture's reliance on drugs to relieve anxiety and depression has at times robbed us of opportunities to grow and has reinforced the notion that psychological development is something that only occurs in childhood. As someone once remarked, a crisis is a terrible thing to waste.

Developmental Change is Facilitated By "Transitional Objects." One of my favorite psychoanalytic theorists, Donald Winnicott[40], provided insights into the psychological function of what he called children's first "transitional objects." Winnicott perceived that toddlers are in the process of leaving behind a "perfectly" attuned maternal holding environment and that the toddler's growing understanding of this is inherently traumatic. He went on to suggest that the toddler's "blankie" or "teddy" occupies a place between infantile omnipotence (the infant's sense that just wanting something makes it comes to pass) and a beginning recognition of separateness from mother and the resulting feeling of dependence on her. Instead of seeing the world as being perfectly attuned to her every need, the toddler is beginning to understand that the world and the important people in it have a separate existence of their own, and, as a result, they may or may not be there when we need them. The blanket or teddy bear (or other object) occupies that transitional space between seeing mom as part of an inner subjectivity and "re-cognizing" her as part of an outer objectivity. As such, the blanket or teddy bear is thought to facilitate gradual acceptance by the toddler that there is an external world over which she has little control. The blankie or teddy is a separate object in the sense that the toddler recognizes that it is not physically a part of her. But at the same time the blanket or teddy is hers, it is completely under her control and is there to soothe and comfort her whenever she desires. Thus, a toddler's so-called "security blanket" is not so much a substitute for mother or, in the terms of behavioral psychology a "secondary reinforcer," as it is the physical representation of the last vestiges of an old embeddedness in a mother/me dual unity, an old belief that the sources of my satisfactions are intimately connected to my desires.

The child's dependence on his or her blanket is an entirely normal way in which the child preserves one piece of its gradually receding understanding of the world, as he or she moves forward, sometimes bravely, sometimes fearfully, into a world of profound separateness. As parents, we intuitively understand that our toddler's attachment to such transitional objects is both important and healthy. So we collude with our toddlers and treat these objects as their exclusive property, and we make no effort to separate our toddlers from them. Both Kegan and Winnicott would agree that when we do so we are being good "holding environments" for our toddlers' psychological development.

A singular contribution of Kegan's theory of the development of the self is that he directs our attention to the existence of similar transitional objects at each of life's major developmental transitions. According to Kegan, Winnicott's blankets and teddy bears are only the first of many transitional objects that help us through the recurring experience of reconstructing the relationship between ourselves and the external world. Such help is useful because at each transition we lose a familiar way of making sense of the world at a time when how we will make sense next has not yet become entirely clear. A description of the transitional objects associated with each of Kegan's first three stage transitions can be found in the following table. (Don't get your hopes up, that new Mini-Cooper convertible you were thinking of buying doesn't show up on Kegan's list.) Each of these transitional objects has one foot in the individual's old way of making sense and one foot in the individual's new way of making sense of their world. The transitional object thereby gives the person a place to "stand" during those vulnerable times when he's beginning to sense that he is no longer who he used to be and the world is no longer what he thought it was. The transitional object provides an island of safety, as the old world view is lost and before he has fully reconstructed himself and the world by using the more complicated "lens" of the next stage. Kegan suggests that there are "transitional objects" that facilitate movement to each of his stages, although in the transitions to stages 4 and 5 these "transitional objects" are more abstract and harder to describe.

The next transition, the transition from the impulsivity of stage 1 to the self-control and self-interest of stage 2, gives rise to a new transitional object, the "imaginary friend." Using this device, two major issues in the transition from stage 1 to stage 2 can be managed more comfortably. The first issue concerns the process of taking a perspective on one's impulses, thus bringing them under the control of an emerging set of long-term interests. The second issue concerns becoming able to recognize that others have interests and expectations that are different from one's own. The imaginary friend is a perfect vehicle for managing both of these tasks. Still somewhat vulnerable to his impulses, the 1-2 transition child now is able to shift responsibility for his impulses to the imaginary friend. It's the imaginary friend who's impulsive: "Omar did it, not me." But imaginary friends can do more than merely act as the repository of the child's impulses. The imaginary friend is also a repository of competing interests. Imaginary friends are notoriously contrary. They often want to do things that you don't want to do. As such they become a vehicle for coming to terms with competing interests, but they do so in a way that leaves the competing interests (what I want versus what my imaginary friend wants) entirely under *my* control. I don't have to figure out what my imaginary friend wants, I know without having to ask or guess. As with a child's security blanket, most parents intuitively recognize that they should be tolerant of their child's imaginary friend, that having an imaginary friend is a reasonably common feature of early childhood, and that the "friend" will eventually disappear from the child's life. Until this happens, parents feel compelled to acknowledge not only the existence of the imaginary friend but also to recognize the "friend" as having needs and interests that are often quite distinct from their child's needs and interests.

The third transitional object recognized by Kegan is the "chum." This special late childhood relationship, first described by Harry Stack Sullivan,[41] entails having a close best friend who is experienced as being remarkably like one's self. Chums enjoy the same activities, wear the same kinds of clothes, have the same interests and goals, and, most importantly, share highly similar feelings. It's almost as if the chum is a carbon copy of oneself. How might a relationship with this sort of "chum" facilitate development from the imperial balance (Kegan's stage 2) to the interpersonal balance (Kegan's stage 3)? Recall that in this momentous transition there is an emerging capacity to *experience oneself being experienced by others*. The other's view of me, formerly an external alternative to my own view of myself, now gets taken inside and becomes a part of my own view of myself. What could be a better vehicle for this transition than the chum? The chum has the same needs and interests as I do, so I don't have to be vigilant to make sure that I get what I want (versus what my chum wants) out of the relationship. At the same time I can begin to make my chum's experience of me a part of my own internal experience of myself. This is facilitated, because my chum's view of me and my own view of myself are, presumably, identical. Thus, I can "co-construct" my experience of who I am with my chum without concern that it is different from my own view. Once the process of co-construction becomes operational in this interpersonal safe haven, a structure has begun to be laid down whereby other more distinct and potentially critical perspectives on me will have a direct effect on how I experience myself. The "chum" thus becomes a kind of interpersonal Trojan horse. The chum seems an innocent "gift" but once "inside" it soon unleashes adolescent interpersonalism (i.e., stage 3) in all its fury. A summary of these three transitional objects can be found in the following table.

OLD BALANCE	NEW BALANCE	TRANSITIONAL OBJECT
Infantile Omnipotence, Subjectivity (Stage 0)	Distinguishes Self ("me") From Others & the World ("not me") (Stage 1)	Blankie, Teddy, etc. – an Object Over Which Child Has Perfect Control – is Both "me" and "not me"
Embedded in Impulses and Fantasy (Stage 1)	Has Control Over Impulses & Fantasies; Sees Others as Having Their Own Self-Control (Stage 2)	Imaginary Friend – a Repository For Impulses & Fantasies That Were Me, But Soon Will Be Controlled By Me
Embedded in Own Interests; Sees Others as Competitors or Allies (Stage 2)	Makes Others' Experience a Part of Own Experience of Self (Mutuality – Stage 3)	H.S. Sullivan's Chum - A Person Whose Inner Experience is Just Like My Inner Experience

Description of three transitional objects associated with developmental transitions during childhood and early adolescence (adapted from Kegan, 1982)

We are left with a vision of personality development that views all human beings as progressing through a series of potentially disorienting transitions, transitions that entail losing a simpler way of experiencing the world and then seeing the world anew through the lens of a new, more complicated organizing process. Each new stage causes the person to discover a more sophisticated way of being distinct from the world while still being in relation to it. Each new stage is inherently more valuable, because each grants to the world more of the complexity that was there all along. At Kegan's sixth and final stage, "stage 5," he suggests that there is a dawning awareness of an underlying unity that transcends human and environmental complexity. This is a view of the endpoint of personal development that is strikingly compatible with some theories in the field of “transpersonal” psychology.[42]

12 KEGAN'S THEORY HELPS EXPLAIN MANY ASPECTS OF CLOSE RELATIONSHIPS

You may find yourself beginning to apply Kegan's constructive/developmental theory to your own experiences. Indeed, the theory provides an intriguing lens for viewing many key features of being human. In 1994, Kegan published a book using the stage notions of his 1982 book to illuminate mismatches between human developmental capacity and the complexity of the demands that society places upon us. Kegan argues convincingly that contemporary expectations for how we should function as intimate partners, as parents, employees, and teachers/counselors exceed the developmental capability of the majority of the adults struggling with these challenging roles. Hence the title of his 1994 book, *In Over Our Heads: The Mental Demands of Modern Life*.[43] Like his earlier book, it is filled with literally dozens of insights about the psychological dynamics of life's many challenges. I have already discussed one such instance, namely society's demanding greater capability than the target group typically possesses. This example concerned "safe-sex" appeals to pre-teens that, as they regulate their sexual behavior, they keep in mind the likely long-range consequences of unprotected sex. Kegan's insight is that lacking the stage 3 capacity to make a future possibility a part of the present moment, pre-teens are fundamentally incapable of responding to this aspect of "safe sex" appeals. According to Kegan, there are many other instances where contemporary society makes what are often impossible demands on our developmental capabilities.

Kegan illustrates this mismatch between conceptual complexity and societal expectations with the case of a woman struggling with her guilt over having lied to her nine-year-old daughter.[44] In this well-known case the woman, whom Kegan calls "Alice," recently divorced, was answering questions about sex posed by her nine-year-old daughter. Things were going fine until her daughter asked her mother if she had had sex with another man since leaving her daddy. Alice lied and now is upset that she violated her value of never lying to her children. She wants the counselor to tell her whether she did the right thing by lying or whether she did the wrong thing by violating her principle that relationships with one's children should be based on truthfulness. Without much success the counselor tries to get Alice to answer this important question for herself. She struggles a bit with this expectation but is unable to discover within herself the basis for deciding.

Kegan's view, based on Alice's responses in this counseling session, is that she is being asked to operate using a stage-4 self-system, when she is still functioning, as are most parents of young children, using stage-3 perspectives. Kegan suggests that Alice is caught between two stage-3 mutualities: a) the conventional idea that a parent-child relationship should be characterized by mutual trust, and b) Alice's concern that her daughter accept her. In both, Alice is co-constructing her experience of herself with an external perspective: a) the perspective of conventional wisdom that one should be honest with one's children, and b) the daughter's potential disillusionment with Alice if she told the truth about her sex life. Lacking a stage-4 self-system, Alice has no internalized system of beliefs or principles that would permit her to step back from and take a self-authored perspective on her competing loyalties. Instead, Alice quite predictably asks the "expert" counselor to be the arbiter between her competing loyalties. In doing so, she demonstrates her embeddedness in yet another stage-3 perspective. If the counselor can tell Alice what to do, then she can feel OK about herself knowing that she has done "the right thing." Significantly, the counselor appears to have a greater commitment to helping Alice become her own decision maker than he does to being the source of her decision.

In Kegan's view, what Alice lacks is a "deeper, *internal* set of convictions" with which she can regulate her competing stage-3 values.[45] This future stage-4 Alice might be able, for example, to operate out of a self-authored commitment to protecting one's children from information that would be burdensome or overly stimulating. If this conviction was truly a stage-4 structure, it could be used to relativize Alice's competing values of being a "good mom" by not lying, and also feeling OK about herself by not disappointing her daughter. These two values would merely be elements in a new (stage-4) view of parenthood. Now she could decline to answer her nine-year-old's question about her sexual behavior without be caught by a concern that she would be violating her daughter's trust. Indeed, she would understand herself as preserving her daughter's welfare in the process of "disappointing" her. This would be higher order functioning, because Alice would be demonstrating an ideology that relativizes and subordinates societal and interpersonal expectations to a *personal* view of parenting. In the parlance of contemporary theories of family systems, Alice would have enforced distinct "parent-child boundaries." Kegan summarizes this developmental view of how a stage-4 Alice, with a new self-authored frame of reference, might respond. [46]

> In the original frame Alice feels there is no answer she can give (to her daughter), at least none with which she feels comfortable, because she is not comfortable lying and she is not comfortable disclosing the truth. . . . But with the question reframed, *whatever* Alice's decision about the usefulness of the information to her ten-year-old daughter, her response would issue from, rather than being an abandonment of, her relationship to her daughter. It is just that the "relationship to her daughter" would now have its origins in a mental context that is larger than her daughter's own expectations or claims upon her. . . . This larger context involves her own "relationship to the relationship," a context into which her daughter's claims can be placed and evaluated.

This idea of a "relationship to a relationship" is one way of expressing the principle that when we evolve to stage 4, we move the structure of stage-3 thought over from "subject" to "object." We have a place to "stand," psychologically, a place where we can consider our connections to others instead of being defined by those connections.

Kegan suggests that the expectation that parents be able to "establish boundaries" in the "family system" is only one of many demands placed on adults in contemporary society. Parents are also expected to take a leadership role in the family by establishing a personal vision of how the family will operate. To do so requires comfort in the exercise of power, authority, and control. Parents are also expected to set limits on their children, even when doing so may enrage or disappoint the children on whose behalf the limits are being set. Similar expectations of self-authorship and stage-4 personal authority are part of modern society's view of how to be psychologically intimate. Kegan identifies six distinct stage-4 expectations in the contemporary literature on close relationships: 1) an ability to exercise psychological independence - a well-defined sense of self that can be brought to relationships (as opposed to being partly derived from each relationship), 2) a capacity to get past a "romantic" notion of marriage to a "recognition that marriage is a partnership between two distinct individuals who do not share one mind, heart, and soul," 3) an ability to set limits that preserve the couple as a primary and distinct subgroup within the multi-generational family system and the larger community, 4) a capacity to support our partner's development from one stage to the next, even when our partner is moving to a stage that we ourselves have not yet attained, 5) an ability to engage in direct communication – to be direct, stand our ground in disagreements, and take responsibility for our responses to our partner's actions and statements, and 6) a capacity to recognize and deal with "our ghosts from the past" - so we keep our own psychological hang-ups from distorting our intimate relationships.[47] All require self-authorship and are, therefore, beyond the capability of many, if not most, adults in our society. Perhaps this, in part, explains the difficulty Americans have sustaining long-term relationships. And, at first blush, this is a rather discouraging view, given how hard it is to achieve stage-4 meaning-making. But there is a solution.

Kegan is quick to point out that constructing meaning using stage-4 self-authorship is *not* necessary for successful living *as long as society provides the structure and support for enacting the required behaviors*. So, for example, if society (or the part of society with which we are identified) clearly communicates to us that we should view significant changes in our partner as expectable and desirable rather than evidence that we are "growing apart" (see #4 above), then we can manage this aspect of long-term relationships without having to be stage 4 ourselves. And that's how things used to work when Americans lived in a more homogeneous society. In the past the culture or subculture within which we were raised and with which we shared our identity provided us with a relatively clear view (at least to a greater extent than seems present today) of how to make sense of and conduct our intimate relationships. Now we live in a multicultural society where we are bombarded with a confusing array of differing expectations about how to sustain long-term relationships. Lacking the internal compass of Kegan's stage 4, we have no way of deciding for ourselves to which views we will commit our loyalties. It is from this inability to decide for ourselves that the move toward restoring "conservative" family values undoubtedly derives much of its energy. And from Kegan's perspective such an approach might well succeed in protecting and nurturing us, as we attempt to deal with the challenges of parenting, partnering, and complex work roles. But what this "basic family values" approach often fails to do is facilitate the psychological development that leads to self-authorship of one's *own* values. What most conservative ideologies seem to have the hardest time doing is helping their adherents move to a position where their members actively question their ideologies.

Here is one place where there is probably a clash of values. I happen to believe that as a society it always makes sense to do those things that promote progressively higher stages of psychological development. But there are clearly elements of society that have a greater allegiance to a particular ideology than to human development. We should not be surprised about this sort of tribalism if, as was argued above, a true commitment to a tolerance of diversity is a concomitant of stage-4 meaning-making. Kegan himself is quite clear about the inherent value of higher stages of psychological development.

> . . . that a given individual may over time come to organize her experience according to a higher order principle suggests that what we take as subject and what we take as object are not necessarily fixed for us. They are not permanent. They can change. In fact, transforming our epistemologies, liberating ourselves from that in which we were embedded, making what was subject into object so that we can "have it" rather than "be had" by it - this is the most powerful way I know to conceptualize the growth of the mind. It is a way of conceptualizing the growth of the mind that is as faithful to the self-psychology of the West as to the "wisdom literature" of the East. The roshis and lamas speak to the growth of the mind in terms of our developing ability to relate to what we were formerly attached to.[48] . . . If this book is about a way of seeing others, its secret devotion is to the dangerous recruitability that seeing (as "object") brings on. . . . what the eye sees better the heart feels more deeply. Seeing better increases our vulnerability to being recruited to the welfare of another.[49]

13 CONCLUDING THOUGHTS

For me, the cognitive/developmental theory of Robert Kegan provides a compelling view of how we make sense of the experience of being human. It is a view that suggests that lurking just under a more visible and accessible surface of individual differences in preferences, personality traits, and style lays a largely hidden dimension of personality development, a "deep structure," that powerfully shapes the experience of being human. It is a view that illuminates the path from psychological immaturity to maturity, of successive transformations of the cognitive process we all use to make meaning. Each transformation is a qualitatively more complex reconstruction of earlier cognitive processes, and each succeeding transformation guarantees to the world more of its inherent complexity. As we progress through each cognitively based construction of reality, more is seen. And being seen, the world becomes progressively more engaging and affecting. Becoming more psychologically mature is not, therefore, primarily about achieving psychological independence. Instead, it is about how, in developing increasingly more complex views of the world, we become increasingly vulnerable to being affected by that expanding world. Those of us who wish to be better psychologists, who hope to better understand human behavior and experience, risk missing what may be the most fundamental aspect of human personality, if we fail to develop the skills needed to discern our own and others' current stage of meaning-making. As Kegan has noted, one of the most important things one can know about another human being may be where that individual is in the lifelong process of constructing and reconstructing the boundary between himself or herself and the world.[50]

Constructive/developmental theory does not, of course, address all of the issues that are of interest to psychologists. Though considerable psychological distress can accompany developmental transitions, the theory is relatively silent about the genesis of psychopathology. Still, the therapist (or caring person) who fails to understand from which stage or transition-point her or his client (or partner) constructs his or her experience of psychological distress is at a substantial disadvantage. Lacking a coherent view of the vicissitudes of normal personality development, we are at risk of mistaking the pain and confusion that often accompany developmental transitions for psychological problems that need to be "fixed." But armed with Kegan's theory of progressive developmental change, we begin to be able to see where another person in distress is "headed" and can thus come to view or journey with them, at least in part, as a directional as opposed to a restorative enterprise. For me there is something hugely reassuring about the notion that a counselor or therapist or even friends and loved ones might be committed to our moving forward with our lives, to becoming more of what we are capable of being and more of what we are capable of "seeing."

Kegan's theory of the development of the self is complex. But then, so is human personality. Over the past thirty years I have found Kegan's theory to be intellectually and personally sustaining, because Kegan's ideas yield many insights about the great complexity of human experience. The theory helps us "see" with new clarity what before we could only see "through a glass darkly." Just the other day, thinking about my seventeen year-old's lack of attention to his school work, I was reminded of a remark his older sister made to my wife and me about high school grades. She was thinking about where she wanted to go to college and remarked with great feeling, "Why don't they *tell* us how important grades are?" We were astounded. We had told our daughter repeatedly that high school grades are a major determinant of scholarships and other opportunities. How could she make such a statement? Had she not been listening, not been paying attention? Then it dawned on me that what had happened had little to do with paying attention and much to do with her developing capacity to make the future a part of her present experience. At the time, she had only recently begun the transition from Kegan's stage 2 to Kegan's stage 3, and her emerging capacity to hold the future and the present together in a single experience was beginning to enable her to "see" a message that had been there all along. If I had been able to understand her remarkable statement in constructive/developmental terms, instead of berating her for not paying attention to what we had been telling her for years, I might have been able to delight in her emerging capacity to be more fully in the world. My hope is that you will find these theories as engaging and sustaining as I have.

NOTES

1. Elkind, D. (1981). Children and adolescents: Interpretive essays on Jean Piaget, 3rd edition. New York: Oxford University Press, p. 12.

2. Gray, J. (1992). Men are from Mars, women are from Venus : a practical guide for improving communication and getting what you want in your relationships. New York, NY: Harper Collins.

3. Myers, I.B., & McCaulley, M.H. (1985). Manual, a guide to the development and use of the Myers-Briggs type indicator. Palo Alto, CA: Consulting Psychologists Press.

4. Elkind, D. (1981). Ibid. p.4.

5. Mahler, M., Pine, F., & Bergman, A. (1975). The psychological birth of the human infant. New York: Basic Books.

6. Kegan, R. (1982). The evolving self: Problem and process in human development. Cambridge, MA: Harvard University Press. p 28.

7. Ibid. pp. 28-29.

8. Ibid. pp. 86-87.
Kegan, R. (1994). In over our heads: The mental demands of modern life. Cambridge, MA: Harvard University Press. pp. 314-315.

9. Kegan, R. (1982). The evolving self: Problems and process in human development Cambridge, MA: Harvard University Press. p. 77.

10. Ibid. p. 89.

11. Lahey, L., Souvaine, E., Kegan, R., Goodman, R., & Felix, A.

(1988). A guide to the subject-object interview: Its administration and interpretation. Unpublished manuscript, The Subject-Object Workshop, Harvard Graduate School of Education, Cambridge, MA.

12. Kegan, R. (1994). In over our heads: The mental demands of modern life. Cambridge, MA: Harvard University Press. pp. 20-24.

13. Kegan, R. (1982). The evolving self: Problems and process in human development Cambridge, MA: Harvard University Press. p. 21.

14. Kegan, R. (1982). The evolving self: Problems and process in human development Cambridge, MA: Harvard University Press. p. 91.

15 . Kohlberg, L. (1984). Essays on moral development, Vol2: The psychology of moral development. New York: Harper & Row, pp. 540-548.

16. Ibid. p.64.

17. Kegan, R. (1994). In over our heads: The mental demands of modern life. Cambridge, MA: Harvard University Press. pp. 360-361.

18. Ibid. p.

19. Feldman, R. S. (2000). Development across the life span (2nd ed.). (p. 389) Upper Saddle River, NJ: Prentice Hall.

20. Kegan, R. (1994). In over our heads: The mental demands of modern life. Cambridge, MA: Harvard University Press. pp. 192-195.

21. Ibid. p. 75.

22 Ibid. p. 192-195.

23. Ibid.: p.82. Rilke, R.M. (1963). Letters to a young poet, NY:

Norton.

24. Ibid. p 311 (material in parentheses added for clarification).

25. Kegan, R. (1982). The evolving self: Problems and process in human development Cambridge, MA: Harvard University Press. p. xx.

26. Ibid. p. 90.

27. Kegan, R. (1982). The evolving self: Problems and process in human development Cambridge, MA: Harvard University Press. p. 223. (material in parentheses added)

28. Kegan, R. (1994). In over our heads: The mental demands of modern life. Cambridge, MA: Harvard University Press.

29. Ibid. p. 304.

44. Kegan, R. (1982). The evolving self: Problems and process in human development Cambridge, MA: Harvard University Press. p. 247. (material in parentheses added)

31. Kegan, R. (1994). In over our heads: The mental demands of modern life. Cambridge, MA: Harvard University Press. p.330.

32 . Kegan, R. (1982). In over our heads: The mental demands of modern life. Cambridge, MA: Harvard University Press. p.243.

33. Ibid. pp. 73-83.

34. Ibid. pp. 115-119.

35. Ibid. p. 217.

36. Ibid. p. 218.

37. Ibid. p. 219. (Material in parentheses added for greater clarity.)

38. Ibid. p. 75.

39 . Ibid. pp. 124-126.

40 Winnicott, D. W. (1971). <u>Playing and reality</u>. London: Tavistock Publications.

41 Sullivan, H.S. (1953). <u>The interpersonal theory of psychiatry</u>. New york: Norton.

42. Wilber, K. (1981). <u>No boundary: Eastern and western approaches to personal growth</u>. Boulder, CO: Shambhala.

43. Kegan, R. (1994). <u>In over our heads: The mental demands of modern life</u>. Cambridge, MA: Harvard University Press.

44. Ibid. pp.87-100.

45. Ibid. p. 90.

46. Ibid. pp. 91-92.

47. Ibid. pp. 82-86.

48. Ibid. p. 34.

49. Kegan, R. (1982). <u>The evolving self: Problem and process in human development</u>. Cambridge, MA: Harvard University Press. pp. 16-17.

50. Ibid. p. 113.

Made in the USA
San Bernardino, CA
23 May 2018